Marie Borland *Editor*

VIOLENCE IN THE FAMILY

MANCHESTER UNIVERSITY PRESS

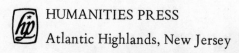 HUMANITIES PRESS
Atlantic Highlands, New Jersey

Published by
Manchester University Press
Oxford Road, Manchester M13 9PL

ISBN 0 7190 0644 9

Published 1976 in the United States of America
by Humanities Press Inc
Atlantic Highlands, NJ 07716

ISBN 0 391 00610 X

Printed in Great Britain
by H Charlesworth & Co Ltd, Huddersfield

Contents

v

The contributors

FRANK BAMFORD, M.D., D.P.H., M.F.C.M., is Senior Lecturer in Community Paediatrics at the University of Manchester. He is paediatric adviser to the NSPCC special unit in Manchester.

SYDNEY BRANDON, M.D., F.R.C.Psych., D.P.M., D.C.H., was Reader in Psychiatry at Manchester University from 1969 to 1974. In 1975 he was appointed to the foundation Chair in Psychiatry in the new Medical School at Leicester University. He was formerly Research Fellow in Child Health at the University of Durham Medical School, and joint author (with F. J. W. Miller, Donald Court and E. G. Knox) of the final report of the Newcastle 1,000-family survey *The School Years in Newcastle upon Tyne* (Oxford University Press, 1975). Professor Brandon has been adviser to marriage guidance councils in Newcastle, Manchester and Leicester, and to the NSPCC special units in Manchester and Northampton.

MICHAEL CHATTERTON, B.A., Ph.D., graduated in sociology from Leeds University in 1965. He was a tutor in sociology at Hull University from 1965 to 1966, when he was appointed Lecturer in Sociology at Manchester University. He has taught courses in criminology and the sociology of police work to police and prison officers for the Extra-mural Department and lectures in sociology to social work students on the university's postgraduate course. He also lectures regularly to courses at the National Police College, Bramshill. Since 1968 he has been carrying out research on urban police work focusing on the police role, the process of criminalisation and the service function of the uniformed branch.

MILDRED DOW, Chief Superintendent, Greater Manchester City Police, is a member of the Area Review Committee on non-accidentally injured children in each county metropolitan borough of Greater Manchester. She has given evidence to the Select Committee of the House of Commons on Family Violence.

MARGARET GREGORY, B.A., graduated in psychology from Hull University and trained as a teacher. Since then she has taught in Manchester in a comprehensive school and with children and adults who had reading difficulties. Her interest in battered wives arose from acting as tutor to a community study group organised in 1973 by the Extra-mural Department of Manchester University. This class chose to study the problems of battered wives, and from this she became involved with Shield, which now runs a refuge in Manchester, and with the National Women's Aid Federation, with whom she gave evidence to the House of Commons Select Committee on Family Violence.

JOHN PICKETT trained as a PSW in the Department of Psychiatry at Leeds University. He has worked for the NSPCC since 1964 in a variety of capacities: as inspector in Leeds and later as a group officer in Bradford, where he was involved in social work education as a field-work teacher. While there he assisted in the development of a co-ordinating committee and the setting up of a register of child abuse. He went to Manchester in 1972 to set up the NSPCC special unit of which he is the team leader.

BERT L. RAISBECK, LL.B., A.C.I.S., teaches law in the Faculty of Law at Manchester University. He worked for six years in local government, where collaboration with Social Services and Education Departments was his special concern. He now teaches law to social work students both on a professional social work course and to social workers on in-service training courses organised by the North West Provincial Council.

TOM TOMLINSON has had wide experience of situations involving family violence. He trained as a youth and community worker and worked at one time in the East End of London. After completing professional training in child care he worked as a social worker for a local authority and in an intensive case-work agency in Manchester. His present job in the Family Welfare Association carries responsibility for staff and student supervision.

MARIE BORLAND, B.A. (Admin.), teaches on the professional social work course in the Department of Social Administration at Manchester University. She acted as a chairman and group leader at the conference at which these papers were originally presented.

Marie Borland

Foreword

With one exception,[1] these papers were originally presented at two
residential conferences organised by Bryan Luckham, Senior Staff Tutor
in the Extra-mural Department of Manchester University, under the title
'Physical Violence in the Family'. In November 1974 thirty-eight people
attended the first course, which lasted two days. They were mainly
police officers and social workers, but also included were a magistrate, a
teacher and a clergyman. The first conference was over-subscribed, so a
repeat course was held several months later, in March 1975, when two
additional presentations were added to the original group.[2] On the second
occasion forty-two people attended, again mainly police officers and
social workers, who this time included a larger number of probation
officers. At both conferences the participants said they would welcome
publication of the papers, and they regretted the absence of contributions
giving a sociological perspective on the subject and offering a social work
treatment approach to the management of the physically abused child.
A sociological view on the contexts of violence is therefore included in
this volume. An account of the social work help offered to battering
parents was, however, omitted, since Carolyn Jones' book[3] specifically
on this complex subject was due to be published about the same time. It
is hoped that the present volume will bring together what is, at present,
scattered information on the subject of battered children and wives and
give a picture of the different views and aims of some of the professionals
and organisations who have to meet and deal with the phenomenon of
physical violence in the family.

Two observations need to be made at the outset. The book is concerned
only with physical violence and its consequencies. Its title does not indicate
that the writers view family violence solely in terms of physical assault.
Clearly this is only one aspect of violence. The verbal and emotional
equivalent which is apparent in many social groups, including the family,
is not seen as of lesser importance. For the purpose of the conference the
focus was on physical violence, and it is this focus which the book presents.

Secondly, one could question the advisability of including two
phenomena popularly labelled 'the battered child' and 'the battered wife'
under the single heading *Violence in the Family*. Are we speaking of the
same thing when we talk of battered wives and battered children? Are the

forces which lead to child abuse the same as those that lie behind wife abuse? Each of these aspects of family life has a very different history of recognition and documentation, and, as was apparent at the conference, they are viewed very differently by the individuals and organisations who become involved with both.

Battered wives and children are the subject of close public scrutiny at the present time. Press, radio and television are continually reporting and commenting on the tragic events which lead to the death of a child. A Select Committee of the House of Commons[4] and a working party of the Department of Health and Social Security are currently examining the position of the battered wife. The phrase 'battered' child, coined as recently as 1962 in the United States, has been incorporated in everyday language and is now extended, somewhat dubiously in my view, to describe the position of the physically ill treated wife. My doubt as to the usefulness of this extension stems less from uncertainty about the phenomena being so different that they should not be linked than from concern about the feelings and attitudes which surround the term 'battered' — feelings and attitudes which have to do with stereotypes about the nature of victims of violence. While it is sometimes conceded that victims often provoke an attack, children and wives are viewed very differently as 'provokers'. It is generally agreed that even non-verbal children can, and do, provoke their parents, but the behavioural and verbal provocation of husbands by wives and vice versa is generally seen as a provocation more subject to conscious control than is the child's and therefore more 'blameworthy' when it occurs. The battered child's image is largely that of a passive victim who cannot escape from a dangerous situation or adequately speak in his own defence. Wives, on the contrary, are not only seen as more consciously provocative, but are certainly not seen as being as passive as the child. They can, it is argued, leave the unhappy home if they wish; they can, and increasingly do, speak forcefully on their own behalf. And often implicit behind this view is a firmly held conviction that some women actively 'deserve' the violent treatment they get involved in.[5] Public attitudes towards 'battered wives' and towards 'battered children' are therefore often in sharp contrast. In rejecting the transferability of the word 'battered' from one group to the other some workers in the field seem to deny 'victim status' where wives are concerned. In effect they refuse to accept that some wives do get injured without any conscious provocation necessarily having occurred and may be just as trapped as is the child.

Different approaches to the child and to the adult were reflected at the conferences and can be discerned in the chapters that follow. In this

area of human difficulty there are still far more questions to be asked
than there are answers available. It seems useful, therefore, to put the
two groups side by side under the common heading of *Violence in the
Family* so that the differences and similarities can be examined.

Documentation of the situation surrounding the physically abused
child greatly exceeds that of the maltreated wife, in spite of the fact that
the 'non-accidentally injured child' has only comparatively recently been
identified and described. Public opinion has changed from disbelief in the
phenomenon to concern that it should be prevented wherever possible.
Failure to offer effective help, often ending tragically in a child's death, is
unhappily becoming a recurrent item for report by the mass media; cases
where help is prompt and effective cannot, for obvious reasons, be given
prominence. Accounts of physical injury to wives are less often featured
in the press. In some degree wife beating may even be seen as culturally
'acceptable', and social intervention is often considered to be scarcely
necessary or even undesirable.[6] The questions asked by the public relate
largely to children. Why does it happen? Why are children at risk not
removed more promptly? When they are removed, why are they restored
to their families, thus risking re-injury? And why, when we are said to
know so much about the issue and have set up special machinery to
identify and deal with it, do public bodies involved in the problem not
co-operate more quickly and more effectively? Parallel questions could be
asked in the case of abused wives, but the remedies public opinion would
suggest illustrate the difference in attitudes towards the two groups of
people. The consensus on children would probably favour immediate
removal of the child when non-accidental injury is suspected; by contrast,
the wife who has left home after an assault is more likely to be advised to
go back and 'try again'. Public opinion, as revealed in the press and TV
and radio discussion programmes, seems to see social workers as going
against this commonsense view in that they appear inordinately slow to
remove children in danger while being enthusiastically supportive of wives
who do leave their spouses. (That the wives themselves do not see social
workers in this light is clear from Margaret Gregory's paper.)

Some of the confusion in this area may stem from two concepts which
are central to social work practice and about which social workers
themselves seem to have very mixed views. There are, on one hand, our
ideas about individual liberty and the limits which society can rightly
impose on individual freedom; and, on the other, our notions about the
'sanctity' of the family unit and society's duty to hold it together. These
are not merely academic issues. How these concepts are viewed influences
the work of both individuals and organisations in the service they offer to

children and families. It also has a considerable effect on the extent to which they are willing and able to collaborate with each other. For social workers, in whom society has vested the right to initiate action which leads to the legal removal of a child from its home, one issue is the social worker's willingness to exercise his legal authority, often against the expressed wishes of the parents. To some this sort of intervention may seem an infringement of individual liberty; moreover it is thought to introduce into the interaction between helper and helped elements which militate against an effective supporting relationship in the future. The apparent reluctance of some social workers to use the powers at their disposal is often hard for the layman to understand. Several of the following chapters indicate that the situation is never as simple and clear-cut as it appears in retrospect. As Frank Bamford points out, even the medical evidence is seldom unequivocal, while the social and emotional data on which social workers have to rely are of a very different order from 'hard facts'. The facts are seldom hard, and seldom do they speak for themselves. Because of the indeterminate and often inconclusive nature of their evidence, social workers are often reluctant to make early quick decisions which erode parental rights. Their reluctance to exercise legal power in an arbitrary manner is surely laudable. The rights of the individual are not to be taken away by the whim of another person, and social workers, like others in the field of human welfare, would be wrong not to respect individual liberty.

Yet the child too has its rights, and if the right to life of one member of a family can be bought only at the price of the erosion of the rights of another, clearly the price has to be paid. It seems an obvious principle, yet at times social work practice seems slow to act on it. Uncertainty about the purpose of social work and about the nature of the relationship between clients and the helping professions adds to the dilemma. One side of social work practice is clearly concerned with the control of behaviour which is deemed harmful to others. But this aspect is often played down or even denied by some practitioners, who choose to see social work as at all times a 'giving' rather than a 'depriving' activity. I have heard it argued that, once explicit control elements enter into the relationship between client and worker, the relationship itself — the matrix from which future helping activities will develop — is damaged beyond repair. This seems to me to be a very partial view of the purpose and nature of the social work relationship. A good relationship is basic to the helping process, but in most cases the relationship is not an end in itself but is instrumental to the achievement of ends. Social workers are not employed primarily to be liked by clients, and have at times to take action on an individual's behalf which puts at risk the chances of being even tolerated in the future. Yet surely one element of social work practice is the acknowledgement of these negative aspects of a relationship, together with the skill to overcome them in most situations. Whether they can *always* be overcome is still an open question, but if respect and care for parents and child underlie the helping process the apparently 'punitive' nature of child removal can be minimised.

The other group of ideas operative in this aspect of social work are those concerning the purpose and influence of the family as a basic unit of society, ideas which are influential when the question arises of the restoration to its home of a child previously removed by legal action. 'The family' as such is the target of much general debate. At one extreme are traditional Western ideas about the primacy of the family in child rearing, both as a biological and social fact and as the most appropriate place for the physical and emotional nourishment of its members to take place. This concept is opposed at the other extreme by writers who see the family as a major cause of child and adult unhappiness. Whatever the debate, the position of the law is clear, and that of social work practice should be made clearer. The aim of modern family legislation, as Bert Raisbeck points out, is not dissolution but reconciliation, 'where this can be achieved'. The aim of social work practice where children have been removed from their own home is also restoration and rehabilitation, not permanent dissolution, but surely the same rider operates: 'where this can be achieved'. Yet some social workers appear to see the restoration of the child to his family as the *only* legitimate goal in child care practice; and when children are so restored, social workers may be among those who, as Sydney Brandon indicates, appear unconsciously to collude with the flimsy stories told by parents to account for the recurrence of injuries. Yet social workers are at the forefront of those in society who daily face evidence of the unhappy fact that some families are inimical to the physical and emotional well-being of one or all of their members and that rehabilitation, while remaining a general aim of child care practice, has always to give precedence to the individualised needs of children and their families. The case for an individualised approach guided by, but not dictated by, general principles is clearly expounded in most social work texts, yet seems in practice to be frequently ignored.

A strong conviction that the family should be held together must be one factor in such situations. The fact that the conviction will vary both between individuals and between the different organisations involved adds to the problems of collaboration which some of the chapters point to: the extremely complex situations which arise when organisations try to

work together in what they hold, mistakenly or not, to be a common
task — the minimisation of physical violence and its consequences in the
family. It is at this juncture that the agencies involved with helping tend
to take up polarised positions. Police and social workers are frequently
seen as having the most disparate views in this field, as some of the
subsequent chapters indicate. Mildred Dow gives a clear picture of how
the police see their role in this field and how they see the social
workers — views which were current also at the conferences. The police
are portrayed as firm, fair, protective of children and not afraid to use
their authority on the child's behalf. They see the social workers as
vacillating, gullible, unsure of their main task in the realm of child abuse
and hesitant to use their authority. Some social workers hold equally
negative views of the role of the police, regarding them as authoritarian
and often punitive in their approach to parents. Beyond these somewhat
bald views lies much complexity of knowledge and practice which, as
Mike Chatterton indicates in chapter 2, is probably completely unknown
to the other disciplines involved and is not shared adequately when they
do come together. Sharing can best take place in an atmosphere of trust,
yet this quality seems singularly lacking in some review committees. As
became clear during the conferences, at many review committees
individuals hold back information from each other, the most frequently
quoted reason for doing so being concern that one group, the police, may
take unilateral action on what they hear at such conferences. Judging
from a comment in Sydney Brandon's chapter, the fear of harmful
unilateral action by the police is not confined to the social workers but
is shared by some doctors. These anxieties, then, represent one factor
which may account for the occasional failure of the apparently foolproof
machinery in the field of child abuse which has been established in some
areas and is described by John Pickett in chapter 4. In some areas the
machinery for detecting, collating and monitoring child abuse has slowly
and painfully been put together. But even when it does operate
effectively from an administrative point of view, it can be much less
effective than it should be if there is mistrust of colleagues for any of the
wide variety of reasons indicated by Tom Tomlinson. Some of the issues
that influence individual behaviour in this field need to be made explicit.
Collaboration never just happens: it has to be worked at. The establishment
of machinery to make it possible is but the first step in achieving some
better service for children.

Whether a similar service is needed for wives is another matter. Certainly
widely varied attitudes to abused wives exist and were expressed at the
conference. At one end of the spectrum of opinion, some see women as

the victims of society in general and of men in particular. At the other end are the cynics who see the wife always as the provoker of the maligned husband. In between there was, however, considerable common ground between different disciplines, which can best be epitomised as exasperation with wives. The feeling was aroused by women whose attitudes towards their spouses were so ambivalent and contradictory that consistent day-to-day help was almost an impossibility. The fact that those who profess to help others do not like to have their help rejected was very apparent in discussion. The very mixed feelings expressed by the helpers, taken with the lack of physical resources (particularly of temporary refuges and long-term accommodation), the inadequacy of financial help and the unfavourable legal situation, made the service offered to wives seem, at best, rudimentary compared with that given to children. But, as with children, identifying the problem is the first step towards making adequate provision, and the conferences went some way towards a clarification of the issues. Whether those involved can help translate the knowledge gained into pressure for policy changes which would provide greater resources for this group, at a time when further retrenchment in social service provision seems likely, remains to be seen.

NOTES

1   Chapter 2.
2   See chapters 3 and 4.
3   Carolyn Jones, *At Risk*, in press.
4   The committee has now reported: see House of Commons *Report from the Select Committee on Violence in Marriage*, vol. 1, H.C. 553-i, HMSO, London, 1975.
5   See *The Guardian*, 7 August 1975, 'Home for battered wives opposed'. A local councillor is reported as saying, 'Anyway, some of these women might well deserve the battering they get from their husbands.'
6   See *The Guardian*, 7 August 1975. A local authority councillor, opposing a Women's Aid request for a house to use as a refuge, said, 'I think they are playing with fire if they attempt to interfere between husband and wife in this way.'

Sydney Brandon *Psychiatrist*

1 PHYSICAL VIOLENCE IN THE FAMILY: AN OVERVIEW

Statistically it is safer to be on the streets after dark with a stranger than at home in the bosom of one's family, for it is there that accident, murder and violence are likely to occur. Accidents in the home are the commonest cause of injury; murder in England, if not actually confined to the family, uncommonly involves total strangers, and about 4,600 children are physically abused each year to the extent that 700 will die and another 400 be left with permanent brain damage.[1]

Approximately half of the murders are followed by suicide or attempted suicide,[2] and among these two groups stand out: first, depressed mothers who kill their children and then themselves in what can be viewed as an extended suicide, and second, individuals pathologically jealous of their spouse who murder as retribution for an often imaginary infidelity and then kill themselves.[3] In the first group the young mothers are often well out of the puerperium and the homicide is most likely to occur early in the illness or, deceptively, during a period of apparent improvement. Prediction is exceptionally difficult, but the risk, though small, must be borne in mind whenever a depressed young woman has sole charge of young children. Pathological jealousy presents risks of a different dimension, and where it clearly exists judicial separation may be the only practical preventive measure.

NON-ACCIDENTAL INJURY TO CHILDREN

Recent public concern has been directed by a series of widely reported deaths to the fatal end of the continuum of physical abuse of, or non-accidental injury to, children. Like self-poisoning or attempted suicide, death is rarely the intended result, but any assault on a child may have fatal consequences. In some the initial, controlled expression of violence escalates uncontrollably. In others 'minor' assault results in major injury — the infant who is thrust aside may fall with severe injury, and shaking the shoulders or slapping the buttocks may in an infant result in fatal subdural haematoma (a collection of blood under the lining of the brain due to tearing of small fixed blood vessels as the more fluid brain moves within the fixed box of the skull).

Extreme violence and death more often involve the father or male
custodian of the child than the mother. Dr Peter Scott (1973)[4] studied
twenty-nine men who were charged with killing a child under five years of
age. Two-thirds of the men were not married to their partner, and half
were not the biological father of the victim. There was a high prevalence
of abnormal behaviour or mental illness in their own family, and twenty
of the twenty-nine men were regarded as having significant personality
disorder. Nearly all of them experienced recognisable and usually diffuse
difficulty in controlling themselves and in coping with stress, whilst no
less than 27 per cent had a previous history of violent crime. Three-
quarters of the men had given unmistakable warning of their subsequent
action but then and later were protected by their partner. In half the cases
there was serious delay in seeking help for the injured child. All blamed
the immediate precipitation of the attack on the child, who was
disobedient, refused to smile or to learn, or was wet or dirty, thus
reflecting his parents' unrealistic expectations of him. Significantly the X
attack frequently occurred when the man was left in charge. In a quarter
of the cases the mother worked whilst the man looked after the child,
thus contributing both stress and opportunity.

Scott described the typical male child murderer as 'a young man of
unstable personality emerging from a penal sentence to cohabit with an
equally unstable young woman who has been deserted by her husband
and left with one or more children. This man is not prepared in any way
for the responsibility of parenthood and, if left with dependent or
apprehensive babies, as is the case when Mother goes out to work, the
stage is set for trouble.'[5]

Many people find reassurance in descriptions of explosive violence by
brutal men, for there is still a great reluctance to acknowledge that a
normal parent may physically abuse his or her own child. Some also
regard the current 'wave of child abuse' as a new phenomenon arising
from our stressful and decadent modern society. There is little doubt,
however, that child abuse has always occurred: what has changed is its
visibility against a background of social sanctions on the public expression
of violence and of rising standards of physical care and expectation in the
community.

In the United States in 1874 a child, Mary Ellen, was discovered
chained to a bedpost, cruelly abused and fed on bread and water.[6] The
police and judiciary were powerless to act, for no law permitted inter-
ference with parental authority, but interested citizens appealed to the
Society for the Prevention of Cruelty to Animals and, as a human animal,
the child was rescued. During the following year the Society for the

Protection of Children was established. In England in 1888 Samuel West[7] offered in the *British Medical Journal* a classic description of the battered child and its family. The syndrome was rediscovered by Caffey[8] in 1946, but until Silverman[9] in 1953 and Wooley[10] in 1955 published their findings there was reluctance to recognise the role of the parent. Kempe[11] in 1962 used the more emotive term 'battered child' and defined the syndrome unequivocally as one of serious physical abuse by the parent or caretaker. Over the next few years the level of concern in the United States was reflected in most states by laws requesting physicians to report suspected cases of child abuse to the local authorities. In Britain the public were slow to accept the reality of child abuse, and it was not until 1963, when Griffiths[12] and his colleagues first reported infants with multiple injuries, that the syndrome gained acceptance — though many of us have vivid recollections of past cases in which parental abuse was not considered credible but now cannot be doubted.

A major milepost was the retrospective NSPCC study of the families of seventy-eight battered children under the age of four years identified in one year as receiving injuries severe enough to need medical attention.[13] In the seventy-eight families there were 106 battered children, 56 per cent of whom were less than one year old. The violence often began with a minor injury, just a scratch or a small bruise incurred during normal mothering activities. The parents were young, tended to have long-standing emotional difficulties and had small families, though often with pregnancies close together. First- and second-born children were at high risk, but where the first was battered there was a strong probability of a subsequent child being assaulted, which argues against a scapegoat theory.

There was a high level of previous violence, and half the men had criminal records. Often the families were highly mobile and were consequently not known to the local agencies from whom they sought help with unemployment and multiple problems, but a significant number of the mothers were rigid and over-controlling, so that high physical standards in the home or in child care are no guide to the risk to the child of assault.

These workers observed that some of the mothers were distressed to distraction by a crying baby and, unlike other mothers, were unable to seek an explanation or offer relief to the infant but directed their attention exclusively to the crying. They noted that some mothers had inappropriately high expectations of their infants and were distressed if the infant was wet, dirty, cried or was unable to learn, and often were afraid to be left alone with the child. Perhaps the most depressing observation from this study was the fact that three out of every five children returned home after injury were subsequently reinjured. A later[14] study based on a national

registry reached essentially similar conclusions, with the encouraging
exception that only 14 per cent of this larger sample were reinjured. The
finding may be a reflection of improved techniques of support for these
families.

Dr Selwyn Smith and his associates[15—18] in Birmingham have published a
series of controlled studies based on 134 battered babies, their 125 mothers
and eighty-nine of their fathers. The average age of the damaged children
was eighteen months, and girls and boys were injured with equal
frequency. Fifteen per cent of the assaulted children died, and 15 per cent
suffered serious permanent damage. Their parents were young, the mothers
nearly four years below the national average age at the birth of their first
child (19.7 years as against 23.3 years), their fathers showing a wider age
range. One-third of the mothers were unmarried, three-quarters had
conceived pre-maritally, but only one-third had considered abortion. The
mothers were often regarded as emotionally immature and dependent,
half were regarded as neurotic, and nearly half were of borderline or
subnormal intelligence. Two-thirds of the fathers had a personality
disorder, one-third a criminal record, and 15 per cent of the partners were
reported as rejecting the child and failing to help in its upbringing. The
father was absent in half the cases where the perpetrator of the injuries
was known.

Three-quarters of the group were from social classes four and five — a
marked contrast with other studies, which have emphasised the wide
social range of child abuse. Marital disharmony, poor use of contraceptives,
poor housing and social isolation with lack of kinship supports characterised
the battering parents. These authors suggest that the failure to adjust to the
parental role can be more simply understood in the context of pre-marital
conception, illegitimacy and marital disharmony than by linking it directly
to harsh childhood experiences.

My own clinical experience has been mainly with the mothers of
abused children, perhaps because of the reluctance of fathers to seek help
but also because explosive violence more often results in prosecution.
Compared with women, the male child abuser is more likely to have a
serious personality disorder of a psychopathic type, and the explosive
nature of his attacks more often results in serious and multiple injuries. A
few fathers have been seen in whom there was no evidence of severe
personality disorder. This type was usually young, often socially drifting
and experiencing through his relationship with the mother social
constraints or burdens he had never previously encountered. Sometimes
from a middle class background he came to face poverty, overcrowding
and bureaucracy for the first time, or found the responsibility of caring for

a small child intolerable owing to curtailment of freedom, incompetence in child care or intolerance of the child's failure to respond in a way he expected. Faced with the care of the child, often itself carrying implications of changed or inferior status, he experienced intense frustration which he expressed by inflicting pain, sometimes on himself and sometimes on the child, by burning, pin-pricking or squeezing. Such young men are immature, dependent individuals, who under stress are unable or unwilling to assume the responsibilities of parenthood.

The commonest group in clinical practice are, however, young women, who vividly illustrate the cycle of deprivation. These girls describe a family life which was always lacking in unconditional loving. Their own mothers had often married young, frequently had serious marital problems, often multiple neurotic or minor somatic illness and were unloving but interfering and controlling towards their daughters. Even after their own marriage — which often occurred early and without full parental approval — these daughters strive to win their mothers' affection and approval, usually in vain. They describe their own childhood as unhappy and often with long periods of removal from maternal care, being looked after by reluctant relatives or in institutions. They often report that they or the other children in the family were battered by one or other parent and that physical violence between the parents was common.

From this background the girls have emerged as vulnerable personalities characterised by immaturity, difficulty in sustaining interpersonal relationships — they have a craving for affection but a limited capacity for love — and a low esteem of themselves as women and as mothers. They marry or cohabit early, perhaps escaping from an unhappy home into an unstable marriage, and before their relationship with the partner can be consolidated they are pregnant. Conception usually occurs outside marriage, but despite their youth and often adverse social circumstances they almost invariably want the pregnancy and resist any suggestion of termination or adoption, which often comes from their own mother. They have childlike, immature expectations of the baby, whom they see as a means of cementing their marriage, helping them to grow up and especially as unconditionally loving. For the first time they expect to have someone who will love them without expecting anything in return.

In fact they often fail to book for delivery, do not keep antenatal clinic appointments and discharge themselves prematurely from hospital. A substantial number of their babies, because of prematurity or other reasonable physical indications, are cared for in the neonatal unit, and this early separation, with its consequent reduction in or absence of early handling, may impair early bonding or create later uncertainty in handling which impairs the developing mother–infant relationship. The competent, assured handling of the infant by nurses in the maternity unit often increases the mother's own sense of inadequacy; the presence of Grandmother or some other capable person in the early days after discharge increases her sense of incompetence and magnifies her difficulties when she is left to cope alone.

A surprising number of these young mothers express dissatisfaction with the sex or appearance of their child and are disappointed by the infant's lack of response to them. After a few days at home they are often left unsupported; their consort is unwilling to take any responsibility and they experience increasing difficulty in coping continuously with the child. They often expect the baby to care for them, and are bewildered by its demands. Adult qualities are attributed to the infant: 'He hates me,' 'He looks at me as if to say, "Just you try and feed me",' or 'She waits till I'm enjoying something, then she starts'. Mothers – and fathers – will say of an infant aged eight weeks, 'He won't let me cuddle him – he pushes me away with his feet.'

Increasing difficulty with feeding, sleep and excretion is largely related to parental expectation of the infant, who is expected not to be 'distastefully' dirty or 'wilfully' sick. The mother frequently seeks advice from health visitors, social workers, doctors and others, who tend to accept the 'symptoms' or 'difficulties' at face value and do not see beyond the mother's veneer of competence. 'Failure to thrive' is common, and may result in hospital admission or investigations which increase rather than relieve parental uncertainty.

These disorganised young women have high expectations of their infants and themselves. Failure to achieve these aspirations increases their sense of unworthiness and inadequacy. They are often houseproud and meticulous about physical standards of care in their home and in the dress and appearance of the child. The baby will have a luxurious pram and spotless linen which may conceal his bruises or, if they are evident, somehow reduce the probability that they could have been inflicted by such a caring mother.

The first incidence of violence often occurs within a short time of discharge from hospital and usually coincides with some personal crisis – a disagreement with the spouse, criticism from Grandmother, financial or housing difficulties. Often the first incident is a minor bruise or scratch in the process of feeding or changing, or perhaps bruising of the mouth due to rough handling of the bottle during feeding. In an attempt to silence a crying baby, and instead of excluding hunger or discomfort as a cause, the mother may desperately close her hand over the infant's mouth, producing the characteristic bruises corresponding to the thumb on one cheek and two or three fingers on the other. Violence once expressed seems more likely to be repeated, and in a few cases a dangerous escalation occurs.

Each incident is usually precipitated by the infant, who perhaps will not stop crying or vomits back his feeds at a time when the mother is tense and anxious. Whichever parent inflicts the violence, it is usually emphatically denied, even in the presence of the clearest evidence, and this denial is collusively supported by the spouse. Episodes of violence often punctuate protracted periods of apparently devoted care and concern often involving considerable effort on the part of the mother. Her expression of affection and concern, *an infant or toddler who responds affectionately to his mother, and good standards of physical care emphatically do not exclude battering,* for the attachment bond between mother and child can survive severe and repeated physical violence.

Though a small group of parents frankly and utterly reject their children, a majority retain apparent concern and affection which makes them at times fiercely overprotective and certainly bitterly resentful of any deprivation of parental rights. Many repeatedly express their concern to ensure that their child enjoys a better life and more affection than they themselves received. This very concern has often led them to break perhaps tenuous ties with their family and social network; the employment and housing situation may increase their tendency to drift, and thus they are socially unsupported and have little opportunity for even temporary respite from the responsibilities they are so inadequately equipped to meet.

Having dwelt at length on the most common pattern of child abuse, it is important to emphasise that a wide range of unique situations may result in non-accidental injury, and each has to be evaluated independently. The following somewhat arbitrary grouping has been found useful in clinical practice but does not cover every eventuality.

1. The largest group consists of vulnerable young women under stress who are immature, unsupported, and disappointed in motherhood. They are often overcontrolled, with bursting of control resulting in episodes of injury. Striking, squeezing, partial asphyxiation or shaking are the commonest forms of assault. Once frank assault occurs there is a likelihood of recurrence. When one child has been abused subsequent children are likely to be attacked. There is often intense guilt and regret. ('When I've hit him I pick him up and cuddle him for hours.')

2. A second group are those with marked hysterical traits. They are very similar to the first group, with escalating anger and destructive feelings towards the child, but injury is usually confined to shaking, squeezing or a hand clamped over the mouth. Then, as aggression reaches danger point,

flight occurs, the child is abandoned and the mother dissociates, perhaps wandering off in a fugue state or more often showing almost complete denial, forgetting the baby and visiting friends or places of entertainment. Serious injury rarely occurs unless the circumstances, which may include well intended supervision, prevent escape and she is forced to stay with the child beyond the point at which she can cope.

3. Individuals who display explosive violence, with other evidence of pervasive difficulties in impulse control. The infant or child precipitates or 'provokes' the outburst, and injuries are often but not invariably severe and multiple. Men predominate over women and the assault is more likely to end in fatality.

One young man of below-average intelligence with previous convictions for vandalism and assault sat his eight-week-old son on his knee whilst his wife prepared supper. He was attending a basic educational course prior to possible industrial training. In the first week he was seriously extended, and resented 'being treated like a kid' by the teacher, who was trying to improve his literacy. He talked and cooed to the baby, who was unresponsive and 'eventually stood up and pushed me away'. Father angrily jumped up, allowing the infant to fall to the floor.

4. There is a group of disorganised problem families in whom violence pervades every aspect of family life. Oliver and his associates[19-20] have described several family pedigrees with up to five generations of ill used children. These families have a multiplicity of social, psychological and medical problems, an endless capacity to utilise services (one individual had been involved with over 200 workers and a list of agencies which covered three columns) and little evidence of any capacity for change, regardless of the resources employed.

5. A minority show frank sadistic cruelty. A young woman, when bored or fed up, would pinch her baby to make him cry and at times inflicted razor cuts upon him to watch his face. When her child was removed into care she invited a neighbour's nine-year-old child into the house and decided to kill him. She grabbed him by the neck and felt intense pleasure as his face contorted and turned blue, describing an almost orgasmic experience as he fell back unconscious. As he was no longer active she relaxed contentedly, and fortunately the boy recovered.

Among those who find relief from tension in inflicting pain on themselves or others there appears to be a gradation from individuals with minor degrees of personality abnormality, usually characterised by immaturity or tension, and who progress from nipping or superficially pricking or cutting themselves to inflicting similar trauma on infants, to those who inflict bizarre and painful injuries such as sitting infants on stoves or in boiling water.

6. Finally it is necessary to mention two groups in which the only factor in common with the previous categories is the end result of damage to the child. These are mothers suffering from severe mental subnormality or psychosis. Mentally subnormal or psychotic patients are subject to human frailty and may present in the ways already discussed but in addition may injure their children as a direct consequence of their mental disorder. An affectionate subnormal girl tried to teach her crawling infant that fire was dangerous by holding its fingers against the bar of a glowing electric fire. A schizophrenic mother heard a voice commanding her to cleanse her infant. She held him under a cold-water tap, then scrubbed him with a floor scrubber.

Deliberately to inflict pain or suffering upon an infant is an abhorrent idea in our society. We tend to recoil from those guilty of such acts, and yet most parents who abuse their children are not monsters. Those who have close contact with them usually become deeply sympathetic and concerned about their difficulties. The parents themselves often find the idea of violence towards their child repugnant and the guilt impossible to sustain, and end by denying even to themselves that any such thing can have happened. Almost invariably the parents unite in collusive denial of the repeated injury. The most serious problem in the management of these families is the way in which the worker — nurse, doctor or social worker — becomes incorporated in this conspiracy of denial.

The evident concern of the parents, their willingness to accept help and their trust in the worker, together with the considerable emotional demands made upon the really involved worker, result in a shared conviction that reinjury must be prevented by their joint efforts. When new bruises appear *even experienced workers are liable to collusive acceptance of the parents' explanation* that they arise from domestic accidents such as falling downstairs and so on. The need for the denial in all parents and the added plausibility of the personality disordered make this an ever-present hazard. No worker involved in a case of child abuse should be in a situation where he or she is not compelled to discuss the case fully with a supervisor or peer group at regular intervals.

The role of alcohol in family violence generally is well known but does not appear to be a prominent factor in the cases of child abuse seen in the clinic. There was one case in which prescribed drugs were a contributing factor.

After a stormy adolescence a nineteen-year-old woman of middle-class background became pregnant to and married an unemployed labourer whose social life remained unchanged after their marriage and the birth of their son. The girl resented the baby, whom she blamed for her current predicament, and as the infant presented feeding difficulties and frequently woke screaming the mother became more distressed. She presented to her general practitioner with complaints of depression, nervousness and insomnia for which diazepam (Valium), 5 mg t.d.s., was prescribed.

About a month later, whilst attempting to feed the baby, she began to slap him, and when her husband attempted to intervene threw the infant across the room and attacked her husband with a breadknife. Subsequently she was overwhelmed by distress and guilt regarding this uncharacteristic behaviour. Fortunately neither her son nor her husband received serious injury and after withdrawal of the drug there was no recurrence.

These paradoxical reactions and other risks associated with benzodiazepams are now more widely recognised, and such drugs must be prescribed with caution. They are, however, useful and should not be entirely discarded.

In considering the steps that can be taken to protect these children and help their parents the first important need is for recognition, and all professionals in contact with young children should maintain a low threshold of suspicion. Non-accidental injury may occur in any family regardless of ethnic group, intelligence, social class or social environment. For the doctor or nurse three D's must be borne in mind:

Discrepancy between clinical findings and parents' account of the accident.
Different, apparently unrelated, episodes of injury.
Delay in seeking aid.

Any one of these must raise a grave suspicion and lead to such steps as are necessary to confirm or reject the suspicion. Even in the face of strong suspicion or even certainty, however, confrontation or accusation must await thorough investigation, the formulation of a tentative strategy of management and the availability of resources for the support and supervision of the family. Area liaison committees with representatives from all concerned agencies, including the police, should now be operating (in all parts of the country) and able to ensure the availability and co-ordination of resources.

If children are to be protected, however, we cannot rely on identification by professionals after help has been sought. We must be willing to receive and investigate suspicions communicated by teachers, relatives, neighbours or even casual observers and accept some curtailment of liberty and confidentiality. Doctors, health visitors and social workers do not have a right of entry, but all have skills in interviewing hostile informants and can usually gain access to the household. Once there, it is essential actually to see and preferably to examine the child. There can be no justification for accepting reassurance that it is asleep or visiting friends. Another visit can be made later, and if the child is still not available or entry is refused then there must be recourse to the courts.

Once physical abuse is confirmed or serious doubts remain, a case conference should be called, involving the paediatrician, the primary care team of GP and health visitor, the community physician (paediatrics), the Social Services Department, the voluntary agencies (e.g. the NSPCC), and the police. At times this may be an explosive mixture, and it is important that an area review committee should involve senior staff (including a senior police officer), as well as representation at a field-work level. The area liaison committee must agree an overall policy and secure acceptance of that policy by all participating agencies. It is unreasonable to expect police officers to fail to act as officers of the law, but the chief constable or his senior officers can satisfy themselves of the integrity and competence of the liaison committee and, once satisfied that good standards of supervision are maintained, can develop a working relationship with the group which ensures that the protection of the child is the major consideration. If the police are unable to maintain a flexible attitude, then the area liaison committee and the field workers may have to operate without the benefit of their advice. Psychiatric representation is useful at the area level and for occasional consultation over individual cases.

Imprisonment or punitive fines tend to disrupt the social and family structure further, and may exacerbate rather than relieve the situation. Probation orders may be of some value as a source of authority, but the powers of the local authority under the Children Act, 1948, are the most effective means of protecting the child. In my view any injured child should be admitted to hospital until plans for the total management of the situation have been formulated. The NSPCC has mounted a series of brave experiments in making social work service available throughout the twenty-four hours, but this is time-consuming, demanding of resources and staff, and despite encouraging early results the techniques remain unproven. Only in a few cases is formal psychiatric treatment indicated, though often the psychiatrist can offer some symptomatic relief to parents and support to workers. Current social work techniques, group therapy and behaviour modification all have a place in individual cases. It is often necessary to take the child into care in a situation where links with the parents can be maintained. Here there is an opportunity to involve the residential care workers of a nursery or foster-parents who intuitively or by training are capable of undertaking the work of training or rehabiliting the damaging parents. By identifying and sustaining strengths and helping to overcome

weaknesses many of these parents can be helped to cope with their
children and to tolerate their angry feelings without giving violent
expression to them. As work with the parents progresses the mother can
increasingly assume responsibility for the child during the day in the care
situation, and progress through days and weekends at home to a trial
return home on a full-time but closely supervised basis. If reinjury occurs
during this process serious consideration should be given to long-term
fostering, and one hopes that new legislation may make it possible to
arrange guardianship or adoption for such children.

The maintenance of the integrity of the family is not an inviolable
right, and there are circumstances in which the parents' rights should be
sacrificed in favour of those of the child. Many battering parents are
reproducing their own childhood experience of youthful, overburdened
parents providing an inconsistent and depriving environment. To submit
their child to intermittent assault, separation in different care situations
for varying periods of time, and then, when the child is big enough to
escape physical injury, returning it to parents to whom it is ambivalently
attached is to recreate the full cycle of deprivation. No parent should be
regarded as untreatable, but social and psychiatric diagnosis should be
considered in structuring therapy. If after a trial of social, psychological
or medical treatment there is no evidence of change, then permanent
removal should be considered, and considered much earlier than is the
current practice.

Once an abused child is removed into care some women, through
neglect or in a deliberate effort at substitution, will bear another child.
The risk to such a child is grave, and society must consider whether some
individuals should, on a temporary or permanent basis, be deprived of
parental rights over any child whatsoever.

The parallels between the vulnerable individual who assaults a child and
attempted suicide is a very close one. Both sometimes have effects other
than those really sought. Both may be viewed as a response to stress in a
vulnerable personality or the overwhelming of a normal personality by
intolerable stress. Both forms of behaviour are more often contemplated
than indulged in: all parents at some time experience the urge to vent
their aggression on their child, and few of us have never wished we were
dead. It does appear that once these universal urges are acceded to the risk
of repetition is greatly increased. Treatment is not a matter of simple
prescription but calls for change in both the environment and the individual.

Perhaps prevention may in the long run be more fruitful. Certainly we
have a responsibility to recognise and prevent further injury to children.
Either by helping the parents to cope or by removing the child to a secure,

loving adoptive home we can facilitate normal development from child to parent and prevent the re-creation of the situation in the next generation. However, many would argue that the situation is more related to current environmental pressures than to early life experience and that there is some scope for current intervention. The youth and inexperience of many problem parents suggest that parent education or teaching on child-rearing techniques in school might be useful. Sex education and contraceptive availability are not in themselves enough, since the mothers often decline to use contraceptive techniques, but there is some evidence that skilled birth control counsellors can improve utilisation even among problem groups. Abortion on social grounds might also be considered, but quite commonly the girls either refuse abortion or do not present to a doctor until the pregnancy is advanced.

During the antenatal period it is possible to identify mothers who may have difficulties in relating to their children, and theoretically there is great scope for education or prophylactic intervention, but it is doubtful whether we could mobilise sufficient resources to tackle the problem. For youthful parents, however, particularly when they are badly housed or unsupported by relatives, we must provide more effective guidance and support. Creches, day nurseries and self-help groups could all contribute to the relief of young mothers under stress, but we must find more effective means of detecting and intervening in stress situations through the health or social services.

We are focusing on physical abuse of infants and young children, but it is important to remember that assaults continue on older children and adolescents. They become more agile and adept at escaping physical punishment as they get older, but by nature or owing to disability they may be unable to escape, and older children continue to suffer and die as a result of parental violence. Those who are able to dodge the blows and those subject to inspection and supervision in a degree which inhibits a violent parent may find themselves subjected to deliberate mental cruelty or stifling regimes which limit joy and freedom. One two-year-old subject to a care order and regularly visited was disciplined by a mother who clearly derived pleasure from a regime which compelled the child to stand in a corner with head bowed and without movement as punishment for such misdemeanours as touching the table when told not to or spilling crumbs on the floor when eating a biscuit.

SOME OTHER ASPECTS OF FAMILY VIOLENCE

Another form of exploitation within the family is incest, which, despite reports by Kinsey[21] and the evidence of clinical experience, has been considered rare. In a comprehensive study from Northern Ireland Lukianowicz[22] reports a prevalence of 4 per cent for paternal incest among unselected female psychiatric patients, and among 700 psychiatric patients of both sexes twenty-nine (4 per cent) had some experience of other forms of incest. Among these twenty-nine subjects the incest was between brother and sister in fifteen cases, a grandfather and five of his grand-daughters, uncle and niece in four cases, mother and son in three, and the two remaining relationships were between aunt and nephew.

Paternal incest was initiated by fathers between the ages of thirty and forty years when their daughters were aged between five and fourteen. The relationship continued on average for eight years, usually starting with the eldest girl but often later involving younger siblings. They were usually members of large working class families living in cramped quarters in industrial towns or living in extreme isolation in rural areas. The fathers were habitually unemployed, often themselves from broken homes, and had usually left home after little schooling to work sporadically as labourers. Of twenty-six fathers studied, all were of average intelligence, none was psychotic, but fourteen were diagnosed as inadequate psychopaths, five as aggressive psychopaths and four as alcoholics. Many of these men appeared highly sexed, engaging in regular intercourse with the victim, the siblings, the mother and sometimes a mistress as well, and similar findings have been reported by other authors.

The mothers were on the whole dejected, feeling overburdened by their large families and by a husband who was described as either habitually unemployed, as an inefficient 'good-for-nothing' or as an aggressive, demanding bully. Eight of the mothers were promiscuous and showed psychopathic traits, two were frigid, three were excessively anxious, one had died and twelve were regarded as without gross personality deviation. They usually colluded with the husband in his behaviour or chose to deny its existence.

Of the twenty-six daughters, eleven became promiscuous and had psychopathic traits such as drug abuse or delinquency, five developed frigidity after marriage, and three of these gave other evidence of hysterical personality disorder. Four girls developed frank psychiatric symptoms — in one they amounted to an acute anxiety neurosis clearly precipitated by the father's continual threats of violence if she revealed their clandestine relationship — and three girls developed depressive reactions with repeated suicide attempts. Only six girls (23 per cent) showed no apparent ill effects from the incestuous relationship.

With other types of incest the initiating partner was the woman in the three cases of mother—son and the two of aunt—nephew incest. All three of the mothers had a psychiatric abnormality; one was schizophrenic, another markedly neurotic and the third later developed an involutional depression. One of the sons was schizophrenic, the next mentally subnormal, and the third left home after two years of the incestuous relationship. One of the two aunts was clearly hypomanic and the other elated and sexually promiscuous. Psychiatric abnormality did not figure prominently in the other relationships, and twenty-seven of the thirty partnerships involving brother—sister incest were free from personality disorder, neurosis or psychosis. Lukianowicz concludes that none of the participants in incest with partners other than the father showed any serious ill effects, and the vast majority showed no effect at all. Of those involved in paternal incest the high prevalence of disordered behaviour confirms the view expressed by other authors that the victims of incest develop character disorders rather than psychosis or neurosis, but in the presence of such gross family pathology it is not possible to isolate the incest as the cause of the abnormalities.

The offspring of incestuous unions have significantly increased morbidity and mortality,[23—24] while out-breeding tends to be associated with hybrid vigour.[25] It seems likely that this biological rather than instinctual basis accounts for the existence of the incest taboo in almost every known society. The strong emotion aroused by its violation suggests the existence of a set of general tendencies that need to be denied. Elaborate taboos designed to inhibit a particular behaviour do not develop in the absence of widespread impulses towards the expression of the prohibited act. Freud[26] accorded the satisfactory resolution of the conflicts aroused by incestuous wishes a central place in personality development but recognised that the prohibition is essentially culturally determined. Daughters are provocative and fathers provoked, but incest occurs only when the normal constraints of the family or of society break down. The breakdown can never be traced to a single source. The fathers may be over-sexed, under-controlled and under-occupied. The mothers may be overwhelmed and at times abrogate their role to their daughters, who may accept it willingly. Indeed, it has been argued that the incestuous relationship often holds an otherwise disintegrating family together,[27] and in other cases the victim secures personal benefits from her acquiescence. Poor social conditions and isolation, either in a remote rural community or in a stigmatised urban sub-culture, lead to overcrowding, loss of privacy and a sense of estrangement from normal society which facilitates the breakdown of normal standards.

Such families commonly make heavy demands on medical and social services, so that the doctor or his colleagues in the community may be the first to suspect incestuous behaviour. However, even among professionals the level of suspiciousness is low. Even blatant evidence is often ignored, and the resulting pregnancy brings the first, sometimes still delayed, recognition of the problem. The law responds in a way which reflects society's abhorrence of paternal incest, and the offender is committed to prison, where his fellow prisoners often inflict their own crude additional punishment for his offence. On discharge, if the family has not broken up, the incestuous relationship is frequently resumed in conditions made worse by the father's conviction. Early identification of families at risk and prompt intervention may offer some prospect of prevention, but the multiplicity of social problems is often daunting.

Such families need sensitive long-term social case work and major efforts to draw them into society. The high sexual drive of many of the fathers, whether due to lack of inhibition or biological excess, may be reduced by anti-androgen drugs, and effective industrial rehabilitation might well be rewarded by a reduction in anti-social behaviour. Unless these family units can be helped to function more normally they will continue to reproduce in each new generation the disordered behaviour of the last.

The children, of course, are not the only potential victims in the family, and recently 'battered wives' have been a cause of popular concern. Again we are not dealing with a new phenomenon, and physical abuse of the spouse is certainly less conspicuous and probably less common than a generation ago. The general improvement in the status of women in our society and higher physical standards have properly focused concern on women who are still physically oppressed. Erin Pizzey has been an ardent protagonist of the cause, and in 1971 she founded the Chiswick Women's Aid, which provided a refuge and in 1973 dealt with 2,500 cases. Her book *Scream quietly or the neighbours will hear*[28] and her flair for publicity have done a great deal to mobilise concern for families subject to violence.

In a careful study of 100 battered wives, most of whom came from the Chiswick Women's Aid hostel, Dr John Gayford[29] concluded that their partners were 'badly brought up men' who had been spoiled or indulged as children and who had usually witnessed violence in their own family whilst growing up. They had low frustration tolerance, experienced extreme irritation when baulked and usually resented their wife's pregnancy. They were often incapable of looking after themselves, and their extreme dependency usually underlay their repeated appeals for reconciliation. Forty-four per cent of the men were immigrants, 21 per cent from Ireland and 13 per cent from the West Indies. Forty-four per cent were drunk at the time of the assault which led the women to seek refuge.

All the women had been subjected to deliberate, severe and repeated injury. Forty-four per cent received lacerated wounds, 9 per cent were knocked unconscious, 2 per cent had retinal damage and 2 per cent experienced post-traumatic epilepsy. The majority were regular attenders of their general practitioner. Eighteen suffered from chronic physical illness unrelated to their injuries, and seventy-one were taking anti-depressants or tranquillisers. Psychiatric advice had been sought by 46 per cent of the women, and suicidal behaviour was common, with thirty-four attempting self-poisoning (ten more than once), seven self-mutilation (three repeated) and nine other methods (two repeated).

In fifty-four cases the men's assaults involved the children, and thirty-seven women admitted that they in turn discharged their frustration in violence towards the children. Twenty-three of the women and fifty-one of the men had been exposed to family violence in childhood. Fifty-two of the men had been in prison or borstal, thirty-three for violent offences, and twenty-nine were unemployed. Gambling was a problem in twenty-five families. Twenty-seven of the women had received private or grammar school education, thirty-two left school with some certificate and thirty went on to further education after leaving school. Eighteen of their husbands had more than minimal secondary education, five going on to university or college, but eighteen were said to be barely literate.

The marriage or cohabitation was often precipitate and related to a desire to leave home, commencing in fifty-eight cases without preliminary courtship. Eighty-five women had regular sexual intercourse without contraception before marriage, at which time sixty were pregnant – fifteen to men older than their consort. All but nineteen had separated at least once, and twenty-five had been battered by their present partner before marriage or cohabitation.

It is extremely difficult to establish the prevalence of the problem, for there is still a reluctance on the part of many women to acknowledge that they have been assaulted by their partner, and there is a marked class bias to this reticence. Women from social classes 4 and 5 are more likely to be entirely dependent upon their husband for accommodation and financial support, and consequently are over-represented among those seeking help from voluntary organisations and statutory social services.

Dr Richard Fox[30] and his associates mounted a community survey in a rural area of Essex and established an acknowledged rate of 0.4 per 1,000 of the total population, but confidential enquiry among solicitors and general practitioners suggested that the true rate was more than double that figure. Approximately 0.8 per cent of all enquiries to Citizens' Advice Bureaux are on the subject of 'battered women'.[31]

The Leeds branch of the Samaritans made estimates in two populations, one of 10,000 and the other of 3,500 clients, and found that approximately 3 per cent of their clients were battered wives. They suggested that the proportion is increasing.[32]

D'Orban[33] established that in a sample of 386 women admitted to Holloway prison sixty-seven (17.3 per cent) had been physically ill used by their husband, boyfriend or cohabitee. In an earlier study in the same prison Gibbens and Dell[34] examined 638 women (a one-in-four sample of admissions): of 350 who had been married or cohabiting, sixty, or 17 per cent, described their partner as violent.

In the course of a study of violent behaviour among long-term prisoners Gunn[35] examined ninety consecutive admissions to Wandsworth prison long-term allocation centre. Using a comprehensive overall behaviour rating, only eighteen men were rated as non-violent, ten as mildly, thirty-four moderately, seventeen markedly and eight as severely violent. Half the married men were no more than mildly violent, whilst 80 per cent of the single or separated men were at least moderately violent – a difference which is statistically highly significant. Of all those married at some time, one quarter had attacked their wives at some stage.

Dr Selwyn Smith and his colleagues[17] found that among parents who abused their children one quarter of the mothers reported that they had been battered by their partners. Two main patterns were identified, namely those fathers who battered both wife and children, and those who assaulted their wife repeatedly, some of whom had accidentally injured a child in the course of the attacks. Convictions for violence had been recorded for approximately 27 per cent of the fathers in both groups. In the second group, where the man's attacks spared the children, it was frequently the mother who inflicted severe beatings upon the children.

Dr Peter Scott[32] established that at least one quarter of men charged with child murder also had a history of wife battering. In a further study of forty men charged with murder or attempted murder of a wife or paramour, Dr Scott found that five out of the seventeen men with children at risk acknowledged child abuse. The pattern of assault in these wife murders was that in fourteen cases battering had continued for a long period, six men had only recently begun beating their wives but there had been a fatal terminal crescendo, and twenty men had never previously beaten their wives but had erupted with a single and fatal attack. The first group of men contained a high proportion of disorganised individuals largely incapable of sustaining any personal relationship, whose lives were pervaded with violence. They represent the tip of an iceberg of unknown dimensions, but from this population the bulk of wife batterers are drawn. Although all levels of education, intelligence and social background are to be found among such men, the lower social classes are over-represented because of the interaction between these personal characteristics and social drift, isolation, poor job record, criminality and other social disadvantages, in addition to the continuing trend for 'respectable' women to conceal their misfortune and the privacy made possible by greater affluence. From the viewpoint of social intervention or prevention the second group, comprising 65 per cent of those who made murderous assaults upon their wives, presents the greater challenge and clearly demands further study.

Compulsive gambling appears with such regularity in any discussion of family violence as to justify special consideration. In most cases the gambling is impulsive rather than compulsive, and other evidence of difficulty in postponing gratification or tolerating frustration may be evident. It is possible that in some individuals the gambling results in the development of such a compelling pattern of behaviour that failure or frustration results in explosive behaviour.

Drug abuse is a factor in some cases, both in the assailant and as a factor in victim-precipitated attacks. The benzodiazepines and possibly some other sedative drugs may occasionally produce paradoxical rage, and this may account for some explosive episodes in men who are not habitually violent.

A twenty-two-year-old student had been on diazepam (Valium), 5 mg t.d.s., for several weeks when one evening, returning to his room after fetching the milk, the door was stiff and he jerked it several times in an attempt to open it. He recollects it almost opening, then jamming again, whereupon he went into a blind rage, dropped the milk bottle and pounded on the door with his fists, finally breaking the door from its hinges. The startled girl with whom he was living had been trying to pull from the other side, and when he entered he began to beat her but was fortunately restrained by neighbours who had by now appeared. He denied any previous aggressive behaviour, and there has been no recurrence since he stopped the diazepam.

The drug most often incriminated in family violence is without doubt alcohol. Many men are drunk at the time of the assault or have woken from an alcohol-induced sleep, and aggressive behaviour is a frequent concomitant of chronic alcoholism. In his studies of alcohol addiction Dr Griffith Edwards[36] has developed a 'hardship scale' which was administered to the wives of 100 consecutive male married alcoholics. Seventy-six per cent of the men were quarrelsome, 72 per cent had threatened violence, 49 per cent were very jealous, 45 per cent had beaten their wives, and 27 per cent had attempted to seriously injure or murder their wives.

Jealousy in its various forms is a potent cause of family violence, for although accurate statistics are not available this factor is second only to alcohol in the frequency with which it is mentioned as a cause of wife battering. Pathological jealousy, or the Othello syndrome, is not a disease entity but may occur in a wide range of conditions, including toxic (including alcoholic) and other organic states, the functional psychoses, and as an abnormal personality development. The morbid conviction of his wife's infidelity comes to dominate the man's existence: he watches her every move, cross-examines her about her current activities and her past life, searches her clothing for evidence of sexual activity and attributes significance to trivial events in his efforts to confirm her misdemeanours. Frequently the questioning goes on long into the night, and he often pleads with her to confess her sexual adventures in order that they can start anew. If his partner, in an attempt to stem the flow, makes a tacit admission, this is likely to provoke a dangerous attack which may end fatally. When the underlying diagnosis is of a psychotic depression or other treatable disorder the integrity of the family can be maintained, but in those cases where the morbid or pathological jealousy is part of a monodelusional paranoid state unresponsive to treatment or an abnormal personality development permanent separation may offer the only solution. In any case the woman should be warned of the risk to her life and steps should be taken to ensure that she has continuing professional support, though the risk both to the woman and to the worker is increased if this is attempted without involving her husband to some degree.

Apart from the clearly psychotic jealousy, sensitive, dependent individuals fearful of rejection, alcoholics who project guilt about impotence or deteriorating relationships, and men themselves having affaires may become increasingly distrustful of their wives and this can act as a trigger to episodes of violence. Constant accusations often have the effect of provoking the wife to behave in a flirtatious manner or to have an actual affaire, but even before this there may be a real foundation for the man's jealousy.

In many cultures and sub-cultures the wife's failure to conform to her husband's expectations — ranging from her religious observances to refusal to engage in prostitution — is dealt with by physical beatings. It seems likely that any circumstances which reduce effective communication increase the likelihood of violence as an expression of angry or frustrated feelings so that Bernstein's[37] restricted codes in educationally or socially deprived families, marked distance between partners in respect of social, cultural or educational background and impairment in either partner may be a factor. So far as the impairment is concerned the effects of drugs are fairly well recognised, but the importance of early deafness or chronic illness is not always appreciated.

Theories involving 'victim precipitation' tend to be resented and usually actively rejected by women's groups, yet it undeniably occurs in many cases of violence of every kind. It is important to realise that family violence is never a consequence of a single event but always has a multi-factorial causation and is frequently overdetermined, i.e. many of the factors would in themselves apparently explain the behaviour.

Birch and Chess,[38] introducing the concept of behavioural individuality, suggested that many later parent–child attitudes traditionally explained in psycho-dynamic terms arise as a consequence of constitutionally determined behavioural traits in the infant interacting with the parents. Frequently parents who batter their children refer to the passivity and unresponsiveness of their infants, and this failure to 'reward' parents' efforts to cajole, comfort or amuse their infant may be an important trigger. In some cases, though fewer than one might expect, the infant's restlessness, irritability and 'uncuddleability' appear to be a factor.

Sexual exploitation, ranging from children assaulted by strangers to incest and women compelled to prostitution, involves those who are already vulnerable in some respect, whose difficulties in sustaining relationships are signposted by a superficial, precocious and often provocative readiness to relate to anyone. Many assaulted wives recognise their role in provoking their violent partner and often predict with great accuracy the eventual outcome. Of those women who do break with their partner a disturbing number enter into another relationship more violent than the first. Obviously the woman with small children and slender resources is a poor prospect on the marriage market and may be unable either to support or care for her children, so she drifts into a relationship with a man who can offer some elements of support and companionship. However, those women who, despite adequate intelligence and access to information, become pregnant to and marry a man who has demonstrated his violence before marriage, survive years of physical assault, then separate only to repeat the cycle with another violent man, must be directed by unconscious motives or maladaptive learning patterns.

Despite our preoccupation with violence in the family and the psychological pitfalls of marriage and parenthood there is as yet no convincing evidence of a satisfactory alternative environment for rearing and nurturing the human young. Despite the hazards, the majority of us survive the diverse experience within our nuclear family to become unique individuals, able to achieve sufficient maturity to operate within our society and to pass on the effects of our experience and prejudice to another generation. This chapter has focused on some of the more spectacular examples of the system's failure, but in the absence of a satisfactory alternative we should consider what can be done to reduce the number of failures.

Adverse early life experience, social isolation and early parental responsibility figure prominently in each of the problems so far discussed. Play groups, nurseries and school, together with adequate opportunity for peer-group socialisation, can reduce some of the impact of an adverse family environment. Where repeated child abuse or neglect is identified the possibility of long-term fostering or adoption may offer the child an opportunity for normal development in a loving, secure environment such as his parents cannot provide.

It is unlikely that our medical, social and educational services will ever prevent the emergence of individuals of deviant personality. Many vulnerable individuals could, however, be given an opportunity to achieve late maturity if they could be protected from the stresses of early parenthood under unfavourable conditions. Quite often the youngster who neglects contraceptive precautions or enters into a liaison with an impulsive, violent man is playing a form of roulette — 'A pregnancy would get me away from home, a less impulsive man would not embark upon marriage at this time'. For many immature girls a jealous or aggressive man is a status symbol ('He'd kill anyone who as much as looked at me') or a strong partner who they hope will protect them against a world they feel unable to cope with.

Consequently the provision of information alone is unlikely to increase the use of contraceptives among these girls, and more fundamental changes of attitude are needed which may be achieved through peer group pressures, examples from cult leaders, group and individual counselling and more assertive family planning techniques. Those who from choice or accident become parents might have been helped by better education on marriage and child rearing in schools which encouraged informal communication in the language of daily life rather than the unemotive language of the school. Antenatal education with opportunities for informal discussion with other mothers under the guidance of an experienced leader is another possibility, but some means of securing attendance early in pregnancy would be needed. The possibility of antenatal prediction of mothers likely to experience early difficulties also needs to be explored.[39-40]

Measures which reduce prematurity, such as abstention from smoking and certain drugs, improved antenatal care and the avoidance of pregnancy until the late teens, all have a part to play. After birth the attitude of hospital staff, health visitors, relatives and friends in sustaining and developing the mother's competence in child handling is crucial. Later the availability of creches, play groups and nursery schools, the organisation of self-help groups for baby sitting, child minding and shared activities can reduce the mother's isolation and provide a needed opportunity for occasional relief from total responsibility in child care. If the fathers can be involved the value of these experiences must be greatly increased.

When violence erupts in the marriage it should be regarded as a medico-social emergency, for the longer it persists the less likely it is to disappear. Community workers of all kinds, including voluntary agencies such as the Marriage Guidance Council, should be willing to become involved in or to arrange family counselling. Where attempts to help break down and violence persists it should be made possible for the mother, and, if appropriate, her children, to leave the marital home with a reasonable prospect of establishing an independent life. This calls for some fundamental changes in the status of women, including the development of a single labour market and changes in the law and in local authority attitudes regarding tenancy.

The family as an institution and as a unit is worth preserving, but when breakdown is inevitable the sooner an adequate substitute family is provided – for children and parents – the better.

REFERENCES

[1] Franklin, A. W. (ed.) (1973), *The Tunbridge Wells study group on non-accidental injury to children*. Spastics Society, London.
[2] West, D. J. (1965), *Murder followed by suicide*. Heinemann, London.
[3] Mowat, R. R. (1966), *Morbid jealousy and murder*. Tavistock, London.
[4] Scott, P. D. (1973), 'Fatal battered baby cases'. *Medicine, Science and the Law, 13*, 197–206.
[5] Scott, P. D. (1973), 'Parents who kill their children'. *Medicine, Science and the Law, 13*, 120–6.
[6] Allen, A., and Morton, A. (1961), *This is your child*, Routledge & Kegan Paul, London.
[7] West, S. (1888), 'Acute periosteal swellings in several young infants of the same family, probably rickety in nature'. *British Medical Journal*, i, 856.
[8] Caffey, J. (1946), 'Multiple fractures of the long bones of infants suffering from chronic subdural haematoma'. *American Journal of Roentgenology, 56*, 163–73.
[9] Silverman, F. N. (1953), 'Roentgen manifestations of unrecognised skeletal trauma in infants'. *American Journal of Roentgenology, 69*, 413.

[10] Wooley, P. V., and Evans, W. (1955), 'Significance of skeletal lesions in infants resembling those of traumatic origin'. *Journal of the American Medical Association, 158*, 539.

[11] Kempe, C. H., Silverman, F. N., Steele, B. F., Droegemuller, W., and Silver, H. H. (1962), 'The battered child syndrome'. *Journal of the American Medical Association, 181*, 17.

[12] Griffiths, D. L., and Moynihan, F. J. (1963), 'Multiple ephiphyseal injuries in babies (battered baby syndrome)'. *British Medical Journal*, ii, 1558—61.

[13] Skinner, A. E., and Castle, R. L. (1969), *Seventy-eight battered children: a retrospective study*. NSPCC, London.

[14] Castle, R. L., and Kerr, A. M. (1972), *A study of suspected child abuse*. NSPCC, London.

[15] Smith, S. M., Honigsberger, L., and Smith, C. A. (1973), 'EEG and personality factors in baby batterers'. *British Medical Journal*, ii, 20—2.

[16] Smith, S. M., Hanson, R., and Noble, S. (1973), 'Parents of battered babies: controlled study'. *British Medical Journal*, iv, 388—91.

[17] Smith, S. M., and Hanson, R. (1974), '134 battered children: a medical and psychological study'. *British Medical Journal*, iii, 666—70.

[18] Smith, S. M., Hanson, R., and Noble, S. (1974), 'Social aspects of the battered baby syndrome'. *British Journal of Psychiatry, 125*, 568—82.

[19] Oliver, J. E., and Taylor, A. (1971), 'Five generations of ill treated children in one family pedigree'. *British Journal of Psychiatry, 119*, 473—80.

[20] Oliver, J. E., and Cox, J. (1973), 'A family kindred with ill used children: the burden on the community'. *British Journal of Psychiatry, 123*, 81—90.

[21] Kinsey, A. C., Pomeroy, W. B., Martin, C. E., and Gebhard, P. H. (1953), *Sexual behaviour in the human female*. Philadelphia.

[22] Lukianowicz, N. (1972), I, 'Paternal incest', II, 'Other types of incest'. *British Journal of Psychiatry, 120*, 301—13.

[23] Adams, M. S., and Neel, J. V. (1967), 'Children of incest'. *Paediatrics, 40*, 55—62.

[24] Roberts, D. F. (1967), 'Incest, inbreeding and mental abilities'. *British Medical Journal*, iv, 336—7.

[25] Lindzey, G. (1967), 'Some remarks concerning incest, the incest taboo and psychoanalytic theory'. *American Psychologist, 22*, 1057—9.

[26] Freud, S. (1901—05), *Three essays on sexuality*. Standard edition, vol. VII, 225—9. Hogarth Press, London.

[27] Lustig, N., Dresser, J. W., Spellman, S. W., and Murray, T. B. (1966), 'Incest — a family group survival pattern'. *Archives of General Psychiatry, 14*, 31—40.

[28] Pizzey, E. (1974), *Scream quietly or the neighbours will hear*. Penguin Books, Harmondsworth.

[29] Gayford, J. J. (1975), 'Wife battering: a preliminary survey of 100 cases'. *British Medical Journal*, i, 194—7.

[30] Fox, R. (1975), personal communication.

[31] Citizens' Advice Bureaux Council (1973), *A memorandum for the Department of Health and Social Security*. London.

[32] Scott, P. D. (1974), 'Battered wives'. *British Journal of Psychiatry, 125*, 433—41.

[33] D'Orban, P., cited by Scott, P. D. (32).

[34] Gibbens, T. C., and Dell, cited by Scott, P. D. (32).

[35] Gunn, J. (1973), *Violence*, David & Charles, Newton Abbot. Quoted by Scott, P. D. (32).

36 Edwards, G., cited by Scott, P. D. (32).
37 Bernstein, B. (1971), *Class, Codes and Control*, vol. 1. Routledge & Kegan Paul, London.
38 Thomas, A., Birch, H. G., Chess, S., Hertzig, M. E., and Karn, S. (1964), *Behavioural individuality in early childhood*. New York University Press, New York.
39 Fromme, Eva, and O'Shea, G. (1973), 'Antenatal identification of women liable to have problems in managing their infants'. *British Journal of Psychiatry, 123*, 149–56.
40 Brandon, S. (1971), 'The mother–infant relationship effects of obstetric hazards'. *Third International Congress on Psychosomatic Medicine in Obstetrics and Gynaecology*, 311–13, London.

Michael R. Chatterton   *Sociologist*

2   THE SOCIAL CONTEXTS OF VIOLENCE

Many recent books and research reports on crime and deviance have drawn upon a theoretical perspective which, in the opinion of those who have adopted it, differs significantly from, and indeed challenges, earlier theories on these subjects. So far, however, little has been done to explore the implications of this literature for those engaged in the prevention, control and treatment of deviants. Part of the reason may be that social workers, doctors, policemen and teachers (to mention but a few) are, in my experience, unfamiliar with these new developments. In so far as they are influenced by any body of formal theory at all it is by the earlier works of which the advocates of this new approach are so critical.

It is for this reason that I want to discuss some of the ideas I consider central to this literature, with reference to violence. I have tried to organise them by taking as a unifying theme what I shall refer to as the contexts of violence. By considering the various contexts and their importance I hope to provide an introduction to some of the main elements in the theoretical perspective which is often referred to as the 'interactionist' or 'labelling' approach to the study of deviance.[1] I hope also that the reader will become more aware of his own and others' conceptions of violence, and questions and issues will be raised which I consider to be not only theoretically significant but also to be matters which, in my view, members of the professional groups I have mentioned should be discussing and debating with each other.

THE SOCIAL ORGANISATION OF VIOLENCE-PRODUCING PROCESSES

Defining violence. The approach I have referred to above requires students of violence to be more interested in how *others* define deviance instead of starting from definitions of their own. In fact it leads us to be as interested in *how* people arrive at the decision that a certain act is violent, and that the person who did it is violent, as previous writers have been in those labelled as offenders and their offences.

Consider the following illustration, which, I hope, will indicate how interesting, complex and important the defining or labelling process is. A few days ago I witnessed an incident where someone was hit in the face by another person who was much bigger and stronger. The blow was powerful enough to cause the assaulted person's nose to bleed, yet there was a policeman standing within a few feet of the incident who must have seen it but who took no action.

If it strikes you as strange that no one intervened I would suggest that certain features of the incident, such as the blow, the nosebleed and the relative size of assailant and victim, were *criterial* to how you defined the incident. They told a story, as we say in everyday language. They enabled you to 'see' the incident in a certain way — as a case of bullying, perhaps, leading to an assault that someone ought to have done something about.

If you did read it in that way, then you could be said to have used the details about the circumstances, i.e. *contextual information,* to construct an interpretation of the incident in question. This in turn provided the grounds for expecting a certain course of action from the observers — which is why the context of an act is of such critical importance to our own response and that of others.

As it happens, however, there is more to it in this case. The incident occurred on the pavement alongside a busy main road, and the assailant, an adult, had called out to the victim, a child, 'Keep away from the road and hold Mummy's hand.' The child had paid no attention and had in fact nearly been knocked down by a passing car. The agitated mother seized the child, roughly pulled her to safety and hit her across the face, causing the nosebleed.

Does this additional information about the context lead to a different interpretation of the incident? I would suggest that because the bigger person was the child's mother, and she had been shocked at seeing her run into the road, it is possible to see things in a different light. (Would it have been different if the adult had been a stranger?) The decision of the observers and the policeman to let the act pass without intervening can now be seen as a reasonable response. *Yet you will observe that the act is still essentially the same as I described it in the first instance.*

What has altered in the amount of information we have about the context. It is the additional information that has transformed the meaning of the act, for some of us, anyway. It is also relevant to note that we can now make an important inference about the 'assailant': she is seen to be a 'normal' mother responding in a normal way to a stressful situation. In the circumstances, we might argue, she did what any other mother might have done.

The example brings out some important points. The meaning placed upon a fact (or an act) by those who observe it (and by the actor) will depend on how the 'naked' act is 'clothed' by details of the context. An act which seems shabby in one garment can look quite noble if it is dressed differently, i.e. framed in a different context. Someone who might easily have appeared abnormal in one way or another because of what she did is seen to be normal after all.

The case is also intended to demonstrate that the observer actively *searches out* the background contextual details which are hung upon the act. He frames it in a context he has built up through this search procedure, and it is his own interests and knowledge that direct the search. Allow me to push the example a little further in order to underscore this last point.

Some readers would probably be reluctant to pass judgement on the case because the information provided so far is inadequate for the purpose. Their interests and their knowledge of human behaviour direct them to 'read' the actions of the mother as a potential clue to her personality or to the quality of her relationship with the child. In other words their training leads them to search out other pieces of information, other contextual details, which we might fail to see because we have not been trained to. If they were able to investigate the case in more detail they might discover additional facts suggesting that the mother was not 'normal' after all.[2]

Thinking about this illustration, the reader will recall how his definition of the incident changed as he was given more contextual information relevant to his understanding of, and theories about, human behaviour. At each stage the use he made of that information altered the *meaning* of the act, although the act itself had not changed at all. Not only that, but his opinion of the woman changed too at each stage according to the inferences the information enabled him to draw.

The perspective I am recommending insists that we must take these factors into account in studying how violence is produced. More specifically, it directs students of the subject to examine:

1   How people decide, with reference to their experience, interests and theories of human behaviour, that a certain line of conduct is violent.
2   How that background knowledge is organised and used to make inferences about the person who committed the act.
3   How they decide what should be done about that person in negotiation with other interested parties.
4   What consequences follow from the course of action they take; in particular, how these affect the person who committed the act and their relationship with that person.

The critical audience groups. The perspective recommends that we pay attention to the observer of the act as well as to the person who commits it. It recognises too that there are certain groups whose definitions of act and actor are of critical importance in deciding the latter's fate. Members of organisations and institutions set up to deal with deviants represent, in their various ways, such fateful audience groups. Research on violence and people officially labelled as violent would involve studying the work of the members of these agencies and their relationships with each other. Pause for a moment and think back to our example, then consider whether we could learn in any other way about how 'violent persons' are produced.

Among other things research would explore how members of these critical audience groups manage the uncertainty and ambiguity in the cases which are referred to them or which they detect. The issues that have to be resolved before action can be taken include such matters as whether the physical symptoms are the result of assault and battery or of 'natural causes'. In the case of an infant, for example, is it nappy rash or the result of the parents deliberately inflicting pain? What does the infliction of injuries by one of the parents imply about that person? When we consider assaults on adults the issues are even more clouded, as we shall observe later.

Besides the difficulties due to uncertainty there is the problem, as we saw above, that groups with different goals, roles and training will tend to 'see' the same case differently and will therefore probably disagree initially on what the appropriate response should be. *The fate of the 'assailant' is decided, in other words, not by what he did so much as by the processes of argument and negotiation from which there eventually emerges something like a consensually validated definition of what the problem is and the best way of dealing with it − e.g. that the man is violent, and that prosecution and imprisonment would be inappropriate.*

The focus of attention would therefore shift away from an almost exclusive preoccupation with the people who are labelled as violent towards investigating the dynamics of organisational processes within the agencies that handle deviance, and the relationships of exchange and inter-agency co-operation and negotiation which cut across their boundaries. This is not, of course, to argue that the person these critical audience groups deal with is no longer important.

The perspective of the 'offender'. Returning for a moment to our original example, one might suggest that if *we* were able to interpret the woman's conduct as 'reasonable' under the circumstances, then she probably felt the same way about it too. We took the view we did because the context provided an explanation and justification that seemed adequate. Suppose, though, that the woman saw reasonable grounds for her action but that we, and others, did not agree because we could find nothing in the situation to explain her conduct. The difference between her view of the context and the observers' would make her a candidate for being labelled 'violent', even though she might have behaved in a way her friends or family would consider appropriate and normal, given their definition of the circumstances.

This suggests that research into violence must enquire very closely into how the person who has committed an act that could be called violent viewed both his own conduct and the circumstances surrounding it. The problem is a difficult one because it requires the researcher to adopt an unfamiliar approach to such behaviour.

For, ordinarily, we are accustomed to assume that such people must be strange, different in certain fundamental ways from the rest of us.[3] It is easy to imagine they suffer from some sort of disorder. To do that kind of thing they must be disturbed, or mad, or inherently bad, we say. Implicit in such a perspective is the powerful notion that they are *subhuman* in so far as what they do is considered to be beyond their own control. We may not be as ready as our forefathers to believe they are possessed by evil spirits in need of exorcism (although at times the view has received a good deal of publicity in the press). But we are often quite happy to accept that biological factors are at work, or subconscious drives, mental or physical deficiences which have constrained them to act against their will, as it were. We consent to the search for other symptoms and the causes of personality defect. In fact we may be involved in the search ourselves, and because we already know the person has been violent it is easy to put together bits and pieces of information about him which, considered separately, would be very ambiguous to confirm the view that he is disordered — that he had been for a long time, only no one happened to notice.

There is a way of looking further than these conventional ideas — which, it has been suggested, are inimical to the kind of research that would attempt to see things from the viewpoint of the 'violent' person instead of trying to find the factors he had no control over. We can do it by reminding ourselves of the critical importance of context and considering some examples of 'violent' conduct which escape censure.

In our society certain actions are applauded and the people who do them are rewarded, however violent they would seem to a stranger from another culture. We do not by any means condemn all expressions of aggression and destruction categorically. In certain situations they are enjoyed (vicariously, in the film or novel), honoured (the fighter pilot who wins a medal for shooting down the enemy), encouraged and even taught (the masculine cult of being able 'to take it and give it out', the disparaging of 'sissy' behaviour by young boys who run to Mummy instead of 'giving him one back').

How different, then, we must ask ourselves, is the 'violent' offender? Is it sensible to search for defects in *his* body, mind and personality when 'normal' people can commit the most brutal acts without incurring an assumption that they must be driven by a pathological urge beyond their control? *Perhaps it would be productive of better understanding if we assumed he was basically normal and investigated his own definition of the context of his behaviour.* Like us, he may appreciate that violence has its value in certain circumstances. The difference is that we interpret the circumstances differently, and as a result castigate him as a 'violent offender', with all that implies.

Once the *similarities* between the offender and the rest of us are appreciated and emphasised, instead of the differences — once we are prepared to concede the possibility that he 'may not stand as alien in the body of society but may represent instead a disturbing reflection or caricature'[4] the way is open to a study of violence along lines other than those which have traditionally been followed. Instead of trying to locate the 'causes' of his conduct by statistical comparisons between 'samples' of deviants and non-deviants — the favoured method in the past — we are led to investigate the *meaning* of his conduct to the offender himself. Direct observation, depth interviews and personal accounts, which can illuminate *subjective meanings* and the *context* in which the actor saw himself acting, are now being used in studies of other types of deviants and could be employed in studying 'violent' offenders.[5]

Earlier approaches which came close to appreciating the importance of the offender's own interpretation of the context of his 'offence' developed the concepts of the 'conflict sub-culture' and the 'sub-culture of violence'.[6] Research demonstrated that the collective meanings attached to acts seen as violent by others encouraged the use of violence by the members of the group or stratum in question. In the theories which explain their origin and emergence, these collective justifications, sub-cultural norms, values and cognitive beliefs are presented as means of coping with thwarted ambitions and a profound sense of injustice created in and by a society where there are gross inequalities in opportunities for making good and where a reputation can instead be made by toughness, daring, skill in the use of a knife, etc.

Later work on the sub-culture of violence has also warned against any easy assumption that those who commit what we would consider to be acts of violence must be defective. It has been argued that this attitude is difficult to sustain if only we broaden the context in which such people are seen. Most of the time they act normally. Just as we do not *condemn* all violence, so delinquents, for example, do not *condone* all violence. Nor do the members of such sub-cultures react violently to all or even most situations. The violence they are prepared to justify, and use without feelings of guilt, will be contingent, it has been suggested, upon '. . . the value system of their sub-culture, the importance of human life in the scale of values, the kinds of expected reaction to certain types of stimulus, perceptual differences in the evaluation of stimuli, and the general personality structure of the sub-culture actors'.[7] The reference here is specifically to homicide. Note the emphasis on the context; on how the actors perceive the situation and on what they consider an appropriate response.

David Matza has argued, in fact, that it is through what he calls 'neutralisation techniques' that delinquents who still believe that violence, as such, is wrong are able to commit what in law would constitute assaults. When conventional constraints are neutralised they are able to see the context of their offence as one to which the law does not apply, so that the act can be justified on other grounds. 'Denying the victim' (one of the techniques discussed by Matza), for example, enables a delinquent to see the beating up of Pakistanis or homosexuals as a legitimate act of retribution performed on behalf of society![8]

Emphasising the importance of the context forces us to recognise how accustomed we are to regard as violent acts which in another context would be condoned and honoured. In the latter case we do not make putative and perjorative inferences about the person in question. We assume that he is normal. But in the former, we assemble bits and pieces of disparate information to confirm a belief that he is basically evil, sick or defective. Research on violence, like that on other types of deviance, tends to approach its subject in a similar manner. Recent work influenced by the perspective we have been discussing has, however, suggested a different type of enquiry, which attempts to get at the meanings of 'violent' acts and incidents for the perpetrators themselves. Sub-culture theories of delinquency went some way towards the investigation of these meanings, but more recently it has been argued that further anthropological and naturalistic studies are needed if the subject's view of the world and of the situations he faces are to be better appreciated.[9]

CRIMES OF VIOLENCE: INCIDENCE AND CONTEXT, AND THE
ROLE OF THE MEDIA

Few people come into regular first-hand contact with what are described
as crimes of violence. Even those whose occupation involves them with
offences of this kind can obviously claim to know the details of only a
very small proportion of the total committed in the country each year.
Yet most people, I suspect, would agree with the statement that crimes
of violence are on the increase, particularly in the more urbanised areas.
I suspect too that most people would have some idea or image of the
typical violent crime; they would feel confident they knew what sort of
violent offence was on the increase. How is it that people who rarely
encounter violence know what 'it' is that is on the increase, that they
have an idea of what 'it' looks like?

The answer lies in the role of the mass media in sustaining and
reinforcing, if not in creating, our images or stereotypes of 'the violent
crime'. Because of these shared images we do not feel the need to enquire
in a systematic way about the context of the offences which, we are told,
are on the increase. We *fill in* the contextual details — where the crime
occurred, what kind of injuries were inflicted, what the assailant's motives
were, what sort of weapon he used, etc — without reference to the facts,
by drawing upon our *images* of violence.

The impression that there is a serious crime wave may be fostered if
the media refer to an increase in the figures for violent crime when
reporting on a particular case which happens to have many of the contextual
features represented by the stereotypical violent-crime images. Incidents
in Manchester and the attendant publicity they attracted provide an
apposite example.

On 4 July 1969 the *Manchester Evening News* carried a report under
the headline 'Violent city: judge gives new warning. Bottle attacks man
jailed for five years'. In the context of this court case the judge had
presented statistical evidence to show that in the first five months of
1969, compared with the same period for 1968, there had been an increase
of more than 50 per cent in violent crime. He was quoted as stating in
court, 'My duty requires me to impose a sentence which will make it clear
to people in this area who use broken bottles or any other weapon that if
they are brought before this court they will be severely reprimanded.'

Like other members of the judiciary, the judge concerned had made
similar pronouncements before, but on this occasion public reaction was
strong enough for several local MPs to express their concern to the Home
Secretary. On 9 July 1969, only five days after the judge's 'dire warning',

the *Evening News* carried the front-page headline 'MPs demand "violent city" probe. Minister in crisis talks.' A meeting, the report stated, had been arranged at forty-eight hours' notice after 'the MPs, in Manchester for constituency and other meetings last weekend, were hit by a wave of public disquiet following Friday's shock warnings about city crimes of violence from Judge Edward Steel'. One member was quoted as saying that he and the other local MPs were concerned about the growth of violence indicated by the crime figures and that they were convinced of the need for 'a government enquiry to find out whether there is any identifiable factor which is giving rise to Manchester's increasing crimes of violence'.

Next day there was a front-page report of a press conference held by the Deputy Chief Constable of the Manchester and Salford Police.[10] He linked the problem of violence in the city with the desperate shortage of manpower in his force and pointed out that the 689 violent crimes up to the end of May that year exceeded the total for the whole of 1966. On a more reassuring note, he added that 'the chances of an innocent person being the victim of a serious offence are no greater in Manchester than in any other city'. Understandably, the reaction of the police was that public concern should focus on the need for an improvement in their manpower position, and that blame for the 'escalation' in violence should not be unjustly laid at their door ('We have the technical assistance, expertise, knowledge and experience for dealing with these offences but we are 250 men short on what is a low establishment'), but they did not want to spread undue alarm. Hence the Deputy Chief Constable's assurance that the crimes of violence which were on the increase might not match up to the popular stereotype.

To offset the effect, however, there had been a feature article in the previous issue, the one that carried the story about the MPs' anxiety. It began with a headline quote from a judge: 'It is a terrible indictment of our times that people are not allowed to walk in the centre of the city without being attacked.' The illustrations portrayed the type of crime to which, the reader was naturally led to believe, the statistics referred. One portrayed a sinister man in a black coat clubbing a male victim, the other was a drawing of a bespectacled woman being attacked by a youth with prominent sidewhiskers.

On 23 July the MPs put their questions to the parliamentary secretary. The paper's headline emphasised that, although there had been a dramatic increase in violent crime, most of the offenders were being caught.[11] The next day the impression of a crisis situation was reinforced by the news that the House of Commons had sat through the night for twenty-one

hours.[12] During the debate, it appeared, the city's night clubs had been
held responsible for the problem. The headline 'Crime leap rap for
swinging clubs. "Night life danger" lashed in Commons' guided readers
to the alleged source of the trouble ('night life') and gave an indication of
where it was to be found (the clubs).

Not every citizen of Manchester would have read all this (although
similar reports appeared in the national dailies), and in the absence of
reliable data the suggestion that it confirmed the public image of violent
crime has to be a speculative one. On the other hand it should be noted
that few people would have been in court to hear the judge's original
comment. The MPs responded to constituents' alarm about what they were
told in the papers (or on radio or television). After that the 'crisis' was
publicised (created?) by news items on the statements and responses of
those charged with responsibility for crime. The responses sustained the
anxieties of which they were themselves a product ('Why should the
experts react so if the offences are not serious ones contributing to a
dangerous situation?') and helped to confirm the stereotyped images
of the context and nature of crimes of violence.[13]

Although I cannot provide systematic evidence of these typifications
of violence, you might ask friends or members of your own family what
comes to mind when they hear that there has been a rise in crimes of
violence. Ask them to describe the sort of offences they think of, what
they imagine happened, where, and between what sorts of people. I
would suggest that prevalent in their descriptions will be attacks by
youths on strangers, usually older people, in the street, beatings-up in
order to commit a crime or to avoid being caught. Even vandalism has
been described to me as one image of the sort of activity that is evoked by
the expression 'violent crime'. Only rarely is death by dangerous driving
included!

Kai Erikson provides a useful statement of the role played by the mass
media in reinforcing and, sometimes, manufacturing our images of the
'typical' crime or criminal.

Today, we no longer parade deviants in the town square or expose them to the
carnival atmosphere of Tyburn, but it is interesting to note that the 'reform' which
brought about this change in penal policy coincided almost precisely with the
development of newspapers as media of public information. Perhaps this is no more
than an accident of history, but it is nevertheless true that newspapers (and now
radio and television) offer their readers the same kind of entertainment once supplied
by public hangings or the use of stocks and pillories.[14]

The people who are selected as material for stories and news reports on 'entertaining' court cases, precisely *because* they are selected and we learn of them second-hand, serve to represent the 'typical' offenders. The cases we read about in the press show us, as it were, what evil looks like, what shapes the devil can assume. Yet they represent only a minority (and an unrepresentative minority at that) of all those that come before the courts.

In the light of these observations I would argue that public anxiety can be seen only partly as a response to the apparent increase revealed by the statistics. More important in promoting anxiety are the societal conceptions of violent crime and violent persons, the images that spring from commonly held ideas about what sort of people commit what sort of violence and for what reasons. They provide the context against which the figures are interpreted. The result is seen as a threat to our values and way of life.

Perhaps if there were a modern equivalent of Tyburn, and *all* cases were publicised, it would correct our distorted impressions of violent crime and those who perpetrate it. One way of checking on the relevance of popular stereotypes would be to explore systematically all the instances mentioned by the judges and the press and record the details of the context of each offence. A thorough analysis like this would provide data for an assessment of the accuracy of the images people are being encouraged to hold. Interestingly, this is precisely the sort of exercise that has been undertaken by F. H. McClintock and his associates at the Cambridge Institute of Criminology.[15]

The substance of crimes of violence. McClintock used data on crime in the Metropolitan Police district to investigate five categories of violent offence: (1) homicides and attempted murder, (2) felonious wounding, (3) malicious woundings (misdemeanours) and assaults, (4) rape and other sexual offences accompanied by violence, and (5) possession of firearms or other offensive weapons. Calculating the number of offences in each category for the years 1950, 1957 and 1960, he was able to show how far the numbers in each category had risen and to establish whether there had been a disproportionate increase in some rather than others.

However, this division of the offences in accordance with the legal categories provided no information about their context or 'substance'.

The classification of the offences according to their legal definition gives some indication of the gravity of the crimes committed but it reveals very little about the quality of the violence and practically nothing about the degree of danger which these crimes represent in the community. To throw some light on these matters therefore, it was found necessary to attempt to classify the circumstances in which each crime was committed.[16]

Realising the importance of the social context and the limitations of the
official categories, he broke down the crimes into six types of attack:
(1) in order to perpetrate a sexual offence; (2) on police officers, etc; (3)
resulting from family disputes, quarrels between neighbours or between
persons working together; (4) in or around public houses, cafés and other
places of entertainment; (5) in thoroughfares and other public places;
(6) in special circumstances. For each of the three years the commonest
type of offence was those in category 3 — disputes in families or between
neighbours or workmates. Second were attacks which occurred in thoroughfares and other public places. The third most numerous class were offences
in and around pubs and cafés. As McClintock remarks, the fact that one
third of all indictable crimes of violence occurred in category 3, i.e. where
there was a prior relationship between the assailant and the victim,
challenges the stereotype of the violent crime as one which typically
involves an attack by a stranger.

However, the increase in categories 1, 4 and 5 needed investigation,
since the rise here was greater than in the others. After all, it is the crimes
under these headings that generate so much public concern. They include
the offences 'in which ordinary people, in the course of their everyday
life, may be attacked by rowdy youths, hooligans, sexual offenders, or
young criminals'. McClintock examined the relationship between offender
and victim further, and found that in more than half the incidents they
were known to each other beforehand or had some business relationship.
In over a quarter of cases the victim and the offender were either related
or well known to each other. It is also relevant to note that in each of
the largest categories, i.e. 2—5, no fewer than six out of ten offences
were classified as malicious woundings — the least serious of all indictable
offences involving violence.

McClintock's findings support the emphasis I have placed upon the
importance of the context, in this particular instance by challenging the
current image of the typical violent crime. He concludes:

The analysis of crimes of violence according to their factual substance shows that
most of the crime is not committed by criminals for criminal purposes but is rather
the outcome of patterns of social behaviour among certain strata of the community.
This form of violent behaviour has increased considerably over the last ten years.
Violent sexual crimes, attacks on police and hooliganism also increased but they are
relatively small groups and the frequency of such crimes is often exaggerated.[17]

As McClintock's systematic study of the official records testifies, the
anxiety-provoking beliefs which are capable of reconstituting a statistical
increase in the number of recorded incidents into a wave of violence that

threatens society can be challenged by a careful analysis of the contextual details of the offences comprising that statistical crime rate. Furthermore the statistical increase which is apparent in a superficial comparison of the crime rates for different years may not in fact represent what McClintock calls an 'absolute' or 'real' increase in the number of offences as such. Other factors can produce the *appearance* of an increase, and they have to be taken into account before premature inferences are drawn. This point brings us to a consideration of the role of the police and introduces another relevant context: that of practical police work.[18]

CRIMES OF VIOLENCE AND THE POLICE

Statistics and the probability of detection and apprehension. From the perspective I shall adopt here every offence can be said to carry a certain probability that the police will learn about it and about the person who commits it. In that sense it is meaningful to speak of an act as carrying a certain *probability that the offence itself and the offender will be detected.*

Almost by definition one can say of the cases which have been detected that they were the ones where the probabilities of detection were highest. The circumstances in which the offences were committed were such that the police had a good chance of tracing the crime and its perpetrator. This may be a truism, but it is worth stating because it draws attention away from the usual questions, such as 'Why did the offender do it?' 'What caused it?' and leaves us free to ask, rather, 'How did the offence come to light?' 'How was the offender caught?' In other words, it leads us to consider the characteristics which led to the detection of the offences that constitute the crime rate and of the contingencies that tell us how the offenders were detected.

Such investigation does not, however, end with the detection of the offence and the person responsible for it. Detection is not an automatic guarantee that an offence will be recorded as a crime and the offender formally processed — arrested or summonsed and charged.[19] With this point in mind, it should be clear that *a change in the contingencies affecting the probabilities of an offence being detected and recorded as a crime, and in the probabilities of an offender being detected and arrested or summonsed, will mean a corresponding increase (or decrease) in the rate of crime and the totals of persons arrested — even if the total population of violent offenders remains the same.*

Clearly these contingencies are extremely important to the detection of violence and the investigation of its incidence in society. They can be explored most effectively through the study of police work. For it is the daily work of the police that produces the crime records and the totals of persons appearing before the courts charged with offences against the person. It is not possible here to examine in detail how violent offenders are detected, or how the police use their discretion not to report certain offences as crimes and to release certain offenders rather than take them into custody. I offer instead general observations on the context within which the police operate in order that their current approach to offences against the person can be understood. I shall conclude on a practical note by suggesting how that approach might be modified, if modification is considered necessary.

The role of the public in the detection of offences and offenders against the person. Most police officers are ready to acknowledge their debt to the public in their efforts to detect and clear up crime. Research in Britain and the USA indicates just how dependent on the co-operation of the public modern police forces are. Broadly speaking, one can distinguish two general styles of police intervention: that which the police create themselves 'by keeping their eyes open and their ears to the ground' and that which is initiated by members of the public when they call in the police. The former, *self-initiated,* style is the type of police work that is often portrayed in the classic detective story. Starting with a set of clues, the investigating officer identifies the suspects by a series of painstaking enquiries, then by more detailed enquiries eliminates the innocent parties to find the guilty person. In everyday police work, however, this style of detection is extremely rare. At the other extreme we have the store detective who hands over to the police a shoplifter whom he has caught pilfering. The role of the police in such a case would be described as *reactive*: they awaited the input of information from the public before acting.[20]

If we turn to offences against the person it can be argued that the police style is predominantly reactive, and, I suspect, many officers would argue that under present conditions it can scarcely be otherwise. They simply do not have enough men out on the streets to be sure that any assault against the person would, in all probability, be observed. But although shortage of manpower is a critical factor in explaining the reactive style, another important point is that many offences of this nature occur in private or in places to which the police do not have unimpeded access even given the inclination and the manpower to patrol them.[21]

Of course, there are alternative self-initiated or proactive styles which the police could utilise if they were licensed to, but many people would see the grant of the requisite powers as an addition to the totalitarian potential of the State. How would the reader react to the notion that special squads should be formed to check hospital casualty departments for patients with injuries that might be due to interpersonal violence? Should casualty departments, even GPs, be obliged to report such injuries to the police? Should the police be entitled to examine medical records? Should local authority Social Services Departments be required to supply information about people with a history of involvement in violent crime, as victims or assailants, so that the police can maintain surveillance and warn men on the beat about the likelihood of incidents they might subsequently have to investigate? Such co-operation and the sharing of what might be considered to be confidential information would enable the police to take a more positive, proactive and perhaps preventive role. It would also be seen as an encroachment on the liberty of the subject, and any such proposal could be expected to run into a good deal of opposition.[22]

Thus because of the low public visibility of offences against the person and because of the legal and customary constraints on police initiative in detecting them through enquiries and contacts, the predominant style is reactive. *To a significant and rarely appreciated extent it is the general public who decide what level of law enforcement they want from the police as regards the assaults they are the victim of or which they see happening.*[23]

The reluctant victim and the recording of assault offences. Even if the sources of information were extended by the type of co-operation just mentioned, the police would still be dependent on the victim to identify his assailant when they had not witnessed the incident themselves. The victim's motives can be seen as another type of contextual contingency which affects not only the level of recorded crimes of violence but the numbers of offenders detected. The following instance is a familiar one.

It is not uncommon for police officers visiting a casualty department in connection with another incident to observe someone waiting for treatment for a bad cut, multiple bruising or a fracture. Invariably the patient will refuse to disclose any details other than to claim that the injuries are the result of an accident. 'I fell downstairs' is one of the commonest explanations. In such cases I have found it highly unlikely that the officer will pursue the matter. From a 'practical policing viewpoint' there is little he can do without the co-operation of the victim and there is nothing to be gained from recording the incident. Because the victim 'doesn't want to know' there is no complainant, and therefore no crime. The incident is, as the police say, 'kicked into touch', no report on the suspected assault being submitted.

Even when the victim is more forthcoming his attitude immediately after the incident is known to be an unreliable guide to how he will feel about things later on. For this reason there is no certainty that the matter will be taken further even where the injury is severe enough to constitute wounding and the victim is prepared to identify the assailant. In my experience policemen are concerned to assess the complainant's motives, not only to establish the reliability of his account but in order to decide whether he is likely to change his mind about a prosecution.[24] This is a salient point, particularly when the offence occurs between people who are related or who know each other well. The prototypical case is the 'domestic' one, a dispute in which one spouse, cohabitant or next of kin has assaulted the other. The policeman approaches it in the consciousness that, however adamant for an arrest the injured party may be at the time, it is by no means unusual for a change of mind to take place subsequently, so that there will be no one to give evidence when the case comes up in the court. Past experience advises considerable caution. If he is not convinced of the durability of the complainant's motives he will try to deal with the situation by other means than making an arrest or reporting the offending party.

Principles and practices of police work. Why are police officers reluctant to enquire further into cases where they suspect that injuries are not the result of an accident? Why do they not always report their suspicions so that the offence can be followed up and the injured party interviewed again when he may be in a different frame of mind? Why are they so concerned about the possibility that the injured party may refuse to testify when the case goes to court?

To answer adequately would take us deep into an investigation of the understanding they have of their role, and into an analysis of the organisational influences that critically affect their approach to incidents on the beat. The following observations are intended to provide only a brief overview of several relevant factors. Space precludes elaboration on them.

1. *The operational significance of crime reports.* Repeated reference has already been made to the crime statistics, but it is necessary to introduce another perspective on the figures by viewing them from the practical context of police work. It is no exaggeration, I think, to say that policemen see every recorded crime as something which affects, and

potentially may detract from, the image of their efficiency. From their
first few days on the street they are sensitised to 'the figures' and left in
no doubt about the fact that the detection rate is seen as a measure of
the efficiency of their unit in combating crime. Since that measure has a
high priority in society at large, it naturally has corresponding weight
within the service itself.[25] This helps to explain why, in terms of practical
logic, there is a tendency to equate the non-recording of a certain type
of crime with detecting the person who has committed it. Irrespective of
whether it is statistically correct or not, the belief engenders a predisposition against reporting an offence if it seems unlikely that the offender will
be caught and if the chances of the complainant following the matter up
are minimal — provided also that reasonable account can be given for not
reporting it if an explanation should be called for in the future.

A related consideration is the fact that by recording the incident as a
crime the reporting officer is making work for his colleagues (the CID
in the force where I carried out my research). They will have to process it,
and if there is little chance of an arrest the investigations only take men
off work on cases with a better prospect of success. For good organisational
reasons, therefore, a not insignificant number of offences against the
person pass unreported or unrecorded, adding to the dark figure of such
assaults which never came to the attention of the police at all. (I shall
return shortly to the significance of the loss of information this represents
to those interested in detecting violent offenders early in their careers.)

2. *Arrests which clear up more than one crime.* Offences against the
person rarely provide an opportunity to clear up other cases by interviewing the offender while he is in custody. People arrested for property
offences, on the other hand, often confess to previous transgressions,
enabling several crimes to be cleared up with one arrest. Even when
they are unwilling to admit to involvement in other offences, searches of
the person and his abode may reveal stolen articles which can be traced to
other crimes. For reasons like these the incentive to make an arrest for
assault is often less than when a property offence is involved. Whereas an
officer *might* consider not arresting the man who has physically attacked
someone else, he is unlikely to entertain the thought if the accused is
caught even in what might seem to the layman a comparatively 'trivial'
offence against property, particularly if there is a likelihood of others
being admitted subsequently.

3. *The operational significance of the injury.* Where the complainant
or witness is reliable and willing to make a statement, and the victim's
injury is serious — as indicated, for example, by the amount of blood lost,
the size of the wound, or his age, infirmity or weakness — it is unlikely

that the officer will decide to do other than arrest or report the assailant. The possibility of medical complications or that the victim might die in hospital will be indicated by his physical condition and appearance. As detectives in the research division often remarked, but for the fact that there were three large hospitals in the area many of the cases which subsequently came to court as wounding or inflicting grievous bodily harm would have been homicides.

The nature of the physical injury is therefore a criterial feature. Provided the victim is prepared to co-operate, the offence will be recorded, and if the assailant is found he will be arrested. Even when the victim is at first reluctant to report the offence and identify his assailant, the police — who often learn of such cases from other agencies such as the ambulance service — will attempt to persuade him to provide the information. Next morning he might be a corpse, and the incident would have produced a murder enquiry.

In addition to these pragmatic factors, the degree of injury is also relevant to the inferences policemen make about the 'moral character' of the assailant. They feel that no one capable of inflicting the type of injury we are dealing with here can be 'normal', in the sense that no circumstances could provide adequate justification. Any claims of provocation are undermined by the inordinate amount of suffering and damage the victim has sustained.

In cases where a charge is brought under sections 18 or 20 of the Offences against the Person Act, 1861, it is therefore possible to argue that arrest is routine in the sense that the injury is usually severe enough to require immediate medical attention. For that reason the injury evokes a legalistic response from the police officer — he does what the law requires. The risk of not taking action to detain or report the offender would be too high, however small the 'bonus' for the arresting officer (or detective) who has to interview him and deal with the paper work.

The operational significance of the arrest and the concern with justice.
Before we can understand the policeman's response to cases where the victim's injuries are less serious than this it is necessary to describe briefly how (in the writer's experience) he sees the arrest and charging procedures. To many officers, taking the accused to a police station to be charged and 'booked up', as they say, represents an additional or alternative sanction to anything the courts might subsequently prescribe. This is not to suggest that anything improper need occur while he is in custody, although temptations are obviously present. Senior police officers have argued that the only real power the police have is the power to inconvenience, but

that power should not be underestimated: to the practical policeman it is
very significant.

To oblige someone to provide personal details about himself such as age,
occupation, address, place of birth, etc, to require him to remain in
custody until that procedure has been completed, to search him, as the
police must do before bringing a charge, and to offer him the alternative
of a night in the cells if he refuses to co-operate is certainly one way of
inconveniencing him. Although it is perfectly proper and administratively
rational, it represents a way, too, of letting him see that there comes a
point when he must accept the legitimacy of police intervention or come
off worse — either he provides the information needed to complete the
charging procedure or he spends a night in the cells. To anyone unaware
of the organisational and legal grounds for it — to the person who protests
his innocence or is outspoken in his dislike and contempt — the time spent
in police custody is an intrusion on his liberty, and the charging routine
is an affront: a demoralising status-degradation ceremony.

The belief that this is how many people see the charging procedure is
one of the principal reasons, in my view, why many policemen are sparing
in the use they make of their powers of arrest. In the instances where the
offence was not serious the policemen I studied would resort to arrest only
when they considered that the offender *deserved* to be arrested. They used
their discretion, in fact, to decide whether it would be just and fair. They
attempted to distribute justice.[26] This interest in and conception of
justice directed their 'search' procedure. They enquired into the circumstances of the offence in order to assess blame. For instance, when the
opportunity presented itself they would talk to both victim and assailant
in order to determine their respective moral character — the sort of people
they were. Had the victim got what he deserved? Was he the kind of person
normal people would find it difficult to tolerate? Was the assailant
understandably provoked?

Where the injury was less serious, therefore, I would suggest that these
policemen can be described as playing a quasi-magisterial role. The
decision whether or not to arrest someone and charge him was made in
the light of factors which the law relating to assaults does not specify.
Indeed, even to refer to such an arrest as an arrest 'for' assault is to do less
than justice to the complexity of the decision and of the search procedure
that underpinned it. The grounds on which the decision was reached were
much wider than the phrase implies — as, of course, they were also when
the officer dealt with the incident without reporting it and without making
an arrest.

It should be observed that some officers disagreed with the style of their colleagues as I have described it. They rejected any claim to a judgemental role, insisting that if there is evidence of an assault and the witness is competent and reliable then the role of the policeman is to take the necessary steps to bring the accused before the courts. Apart from underlining the various styles of policing which may be found in any one police division, let alone a police force, this also reminds us of an earlier point: that *whether someone is proceeded against for an assault will depend not so much on what he has done as on the style of the police officer dealing with the incident and the contextual details he considers to be significant.*

SUMMARY AND DISCUSSION

Although it has been possible to provide only a brief sketch of the background to police decisions which lead to someone appearing before the courts, we can now bring together several of the points raised earlier.

It will be observed that in studying how the policeman responds to an incident where there is *prima facie* evidence that a criminal assault has taken place I adopted the approach recommended at the beginning. It was necessary to investigate the experiences, knowledge and interests of policemen, for example their concern with the crime figures; their understanding of the arrest and charge procedures, which gave the act of arrest a significance that civilians would fail to appreciate; and the interest in distributive justice which led them to investigate whether it was fair to arrest an alleged assailant. It was possible to begin to understand the way a police officer 'clothes' the act of assault with contextual details related to these central interests. His search procedure comprises, in part, an attempt to establish the moral character of the victim and the assailant, using clues and signs which we would certainly not find indicated in the law, or indeed in the evidence subsequently given in court to justify taking the accused into custody.

As was indicated earlier, without a careful analysis of how decisions are made we cannot begin to understand how a population of violent offenders, i.e. people arrested and prosecuted for violent crimes, comes to be produced. The study of police work provides an instance of how significant the labelling process is to the study of deviance — in this particular instance, violence.

It was noted that a statistical increase in the crime rate could be produced by any change in the contingencies affecting the probability of detection and apprehension. Our comments on police work have identified several of those contingencies. In view of the dependence of the police on the public, and particularly on the victims of assault bringing offences to their notice, it should now be apparent that if members of the public become more concerned about violence, and if that concern predisposes them to report assaults which might formerly have gone unreported and unrecorded, then this in itself will produce an increase in the rate of violent crime. Ironically they will then be contributing to the very anxieties which prompted them to report more incidents in the first place. If still more offences are reported, public anxiety may grow greater, and so on in a vicious spiral.

It can be said without fear of contradiction that collectively the police know of more 'violent' incidents than they report. Once the fact is appreciated it raises a number of important issues which entail consideration of the role of the police in relation to violence but which also demand an honest and searching appraisal of the present and prospective roles of other agencies. I would suggest that until this latter issue has been fully debated and recommendations have emerged, it will be difficult to provide a rationale for changing the practices which have been described.

What do the personnel in these other agencies consider to be the sort of violence with which they should be involved? What kind of violence would a person have to commit before he qualified for help, guidance and treatment? Are the grounds on which he qualifies, and which are believed to distinguish him from the other 'violent' offenders who have been discussed above and with whom the police come into contact, really as reliable and convincing as we tend to assume?

It might be argued, for instance, that a genuine commitment to the prevention of violence requires intervention at an early stage by people who are qualified to help — intervention when the degree of injury may not be serious and when there is 'blame' on both sides. For the reasons I have indicated, cases which could be dealt with in this way are unlikely at present to be reported, and this highlights the importance to any effective violence prevention programme of utilising the vast amount of knowledge which the operational police officer carries around in his head.

At various points reference has been made to the obstacles in the way of greater co-operation between the agencies which might be more effectively involved in this field. As far as the police are concerned I would argue, in conclusion, that they would have to reorientate their approach in certain respects in order to appreciate that by reporting the assailant who perhaps was justifiably provoked they would not be 'doing him down', perpetrating an injustice, but providing him with qualified help. Some ideas about the value of information would have to be revised. Consideration would be needed of other purposes to which information about an offence could be put, even if the victim appears not to be interested in prosecuting the assailant.

Before the policeman is prepared to act as 'the eyes and ears' of such agencies and adopt an even broader service role, however, he will need to be convinced, and no doubt rightly so, that they have an effective contribution to make and that their approach can achieve more than the one he is accustomed to adopting. That is another reason why, as I have argued throughout this chapter, appraisal and study of the role of the other critical audience groups is so necessary both to the analysis of violence and to the development of programmes aimed at preventing it.

NOTES

[1] For a more detailed introduction to this approach and illustrations of its research applications see Becker (1963, 1964), Cicourel (1968), Cohen (1971, 1973), Emerson (1969), Erikson (1966), Lemert (1967), Matza (1969), Rock and McIntosh (1974), Rubington and Weinberg (1968), Schur (1965, 1971), Scott (1969) and Young (1971). For criticism and appraisal see Box (1971), Coulter (1973), Taylor *et al.* (1973) and Gibbs (1966).

[2] Again, if we were to learn subsequently that the mother had seriously assaulted her child a few weeks after the incident and was labelled as a violent person we could 're-read' the incident as documenting the fact that 'she had been that way all along'. In the literature on deviance this process is referred to as 'retrospective interpretation'. See, for example, John Kitsuse, 'Societal reaction to deviant behaviour: problems of theory and method', in Becker (1964), p. 96. Goffman (1968) also refers to similar processes of definition in total institutions, e.g. prisons or mental hospitals. For example, he describes 'the interpretive scheme' of the staff in such institutions operating 'as soon as the inmate enters, the staff having the notion that entrance is *prima facie* evidence that one must be the kind of person the institution was set up to handle . . . a man in a mental hospital must be sick. If not . . . sick, why else would he be there?' (p. 81). He explains that the responses which the inmate may make to what he considers personal affronts and assaults upon his self-conception are interpreted by 'the interpretive scheme' of the staff body as evidence of the patient's problem, which calls forth a further attack on his identity. This process Goffman calls 'looping' (p. 41).

[3] For an extended discussion of this point and criticism of earlier theories on juvenile delinquency in particular see Matza (1964), especially chapter I; Sykes and Matza (1957); Matza and Sykes (1961).

[4] Matza and Sykes (1961), p. 717.

[5] Schur (1971), p. 12.

[6] See, for example, Cloward and Ohlin (1961), and, for a review and critical appraisal of sub-cultural theories of juvenile delinquency with reference to data on Britain, Downes (1966).

[7] Wolfgang and Ferracuti (1967), p. 152.

8   Matza (1964).
9   See especially Matza (1969).
10   *Manchester Evening News,* 10 July 1969.
11   *Ibid.,* 23 July 1969.
12   *Ibid.,* 24 July 1969.
13   Cohen (1973) examines the critical role of the mass media in creating such moral panics and folk devils with reference to the 'mods and rockers' phenomenon.
14   Kai Erikson, in Becker (1964), p. 14.
15   McClintock (1963).
16   *Ibid.,* p. 27.
17   *Ibid.,* p. 57.
18   Cf. '. . . in the absence of precise knowledge of police work it is necessary to be extremely cautious in the interpretation of changes that may occur in the statistics on indictable offences against the person' (McClintock, 1963, p. 61).
19   The importance of distinguishing between the probabilities of detection and of sanction has also been stressed by Black and Reiss (1970) and Black (1970).
20   These two styles of police work were first discussed in Albert Reiss and David Bordua, 'Environment and organisation: a perspective on the police', in Bordua (1967). See also Black and Reiss (1970) and Reiss (1971).
21   Stinchcombe (1963).
22   Skolnick (1966).
23   The ideas presented in this section on police work were developed from over 1,000 hours spent on research on the police in a territorial division of a city police force in the north of England. The writer patrolled with members of the uniformed branch and spent some time with the CID. Statistical data were also collected on the arrests effected on the division during the research period. Although the data refer to an earlier period (1968–70), the discussions with police officers since that period suggest that the general observations and conclusion are still valid.

I would like to express my thanks to the Social Science Research Council for financing a large part of the research and to the chief constable and his staff in the police force where I concluded the study for their co-operation and assistance.
24   Cf. Jerome Skolnick and J. Richard Woodworth 'Bureaucracy, information and social control: a study of a morals detail', in Bordua (1967), *op. cit.*
25   Skolnick (1966).
26   Cf. Banton (1964), Wilson (1968).

REFERENCES

Banton, M. (1964), *The Policeman in the Community,* London, Tavistock.
Becker, H. S. (1963), *Outsiders: Studies in the Sociology of Deviance,* New York, Free Press.
— (ed.) (1964), *The Other Side: Perspectives on Deviance,* New York, Free Press.
Black, D. (1970), 'Production of crime rates', *American Sociological Review,* vol. 36, pp. 733–47.
Black, D., and Reiss, A. (1970), 'Police control of juveniles', *American Sociological Review,* vol. 35, pp. 63–7.
Box, S. (1971), *Deviance, Reality and Society,* London, Holt Rinehart & Winston.

Bordua, D. (ed.) (1967), *The Police,* London, Wiley.

Cicourel, A. (1968), *The Social Organisation of Juvenile Justice,* London, Wiley.

Cloward, R., and Ohlin, L. (1961), *Delinquency and Opportunity,* London, Routledge & Kegan Paul.

Cohen, S. (ed.) (1971), *Images of Deviance,* Harmondsworth, Penguin.

— (1973), *Folk Devils and Moral Panics,* St Albans, Paladin.

Coulter, J. (1973), *Approaches to Insanity,* London, Martin Robertson.

Downes, D. (1966), *The Delinquent Solution,* London, Routledge & Kegan Paul.

Emerson, R. (1969), *Judging Delinquents: Context and Process in Juvenile Court,* Chicago, Aldine.

Erikson, K. (1966), *Wayward Puritans: a Study in the Sociology of Deviance,* London, Wiley.

Gibbs, J. (1966), 'Conceptions of deviant behaviour: the old and the new', *Pacific Sociological Review,* vol. 9, spring.

Goffman, E. (1968), *Asylums,* Harmondsworth, Penguin.

Lemert, E. (1967), *Human Deviance, Social Problems and Social Control,* Englewood Cliffs, N.J., Prentice-Hall.

Matza, D. (1964), *Delinquency and Drift,* London, Wiley.

— (1969), *Becoming Deviant,* Englewood Cliffs, N.J., Prentice-Hall.

Matza, D., and Sykes, G. (1961), 'Juvenile delinquency and subterranean values', *American Sociological Review,* vol. 26, pp. 712–29.

McClintock, F. H. (1963), *Crimes of Violence,* London, Macmillan.

Reiss, A. (1971), *The Police and the Public,* London, Yale University Press.

Rock, P., and McIntosh, M. (1974), *Deviance and Social Control,* London, Tavistock.

Rubington, E., and Weinberg, M. (1968), *Deviance: the Interactionist Perspective,* London, Collier-Macmillan.

Schur, E. (1965), *Crimes without Victims,* Englewood Cliffs, N.J., Prentice-Hall.

— (1971), *Labelling Deviant Behaviour,* London, Harper & Row.

Scott, R. (1969), *The Making of Blind Men,* New York, Russell Sage.

Skolnick, J. (1966), *Justice without Trial,* London, Wiley.

Stinchcombe, A. (1963), 'Institutions of privacy in the determination of police administrative practice', *American Journal of Sociology,* vol. 69, September.

Sykes, G., and Matza, D. (1957), 'Techniques of neutralisation', *American Sociological Review,* vol. 22, pp. 664–70.

Taylor, I., Walton, P., and Young, J. (1973), *The New Criminology,* London, Routledge & Kegan Paul.

Wilson, J. Q. (1968), *Varieties of Police Behaviour,* Cambridge, Mass., Harvard University Press.

Wolfgang, M., and Ferracuti, F. (1967), *The Sub-culture of Violence,* London, Tavistock.

Young, J. (1971), *The Drugtakers: the Social Meaning of Drug Abuse,* London, Paladin.

Frank N. Bamford   *Paediatrician*

3   MEDICAL DIAGNOSIS IN NON-ACCIDENTAL INJURY OF CHILDREN

The recognition of child abuse is a responsibility of the public in general and of several professions in particular, but medical personnel have special duties in diagnosis. Others have their part to play, but in deciding about the cause and extent of injuries medical expertise and technology are often of critical importance. It should be understood, however, that the diagnosis of non-accidental trauma is an opinion based upon the interpretation of osberved abnormalities in the child and is not susceptible to absolute scientific proof. Neither does it alone constitute legal proof of the need for protection or of an offence. The confidence that can be placed in the medical opinion and the weight that should be given to it varies with the nature of the injuries, and it is the purpose of this chapter to review them.

PRESENTING COMPLAINT

The way that non-accidental trauma is drawn to medical attention largely depends upon its type and severity. It can be classified as follows:

1   Serious and life-threatening.
2   Not so serious but obviously requiring treatment.
3   Not serious and not apparently requiring treatment.

Children with life-threatening injuries are almost always taken directly to casualty departments of hospitals. They are usually either unconscious or collapsed owing to shock, and on arrival some are found to be dead. A few children present with convulsions and some attend because of burns.
   Less severely injured children may be taken to hospital or to their family doctors. There is often a complaint that the child has lost the use of a limb or that it is swollen or deformed. Refusal of food, vomiting or excessive crying are sometimes the presenting problem, and trauma may not be discovered until after the child has been admitted to a paediatric ward.
   It is unusual for parents to consult their doctors about non-accidental bruising or injuries not obviously requiring treatment. Medical advice is

sought as a result of complaints by teachers, child minders or relatives. In addition such injuries may be found during routine medical examinations, especially those carried out when children are admitted to the care of local authorities. The number of requests for an opinion about the interpretation of minor injuries has greatly increased in recent years, and this presumably stems from a greater public awareness of child abuse.

THE HISTORY

The quality of the history obtained when a child is brought for medical attention varies with the attitude of the parents. It is valuable irrespective of its factual accuracy, and the manner in which it is given is particularly important. Some parents are overtly anxious or full of remorse, and give an effusive and fairly accurate account of what has happened. Others show scant concern and do not accompany their children to hospital but send them with older brothers or sisters. Nonchalance and a denial of any knowledge of the injuries is a similar reaction that is sometimes encountered. Collusion between the two parents is usual, but when there has been a marital dispute — and especially when the wife has been battered — her account of the assault on her child is likely to be exaggerated. The majority of parents, however, are suspicious, and history taking is difficult. They tend to delay seeking medical treatment for their children, and often give explanations that are seriously inconsistent with the extent of the damage to their child. Unlikely reasons for major injuries that are commonly advanced are falls from a bed or tipping of the pram.

Previous injuries are often concealed, and treatment may have been obtained at several different hospitals in the past. It is important, therefore, that this part of the history should be cross-checked, and information should be sought about any orthopaedic care received by the child or by other children in the family. Accounts of past hospital admissions for non-traumatic conditions are more readily forthcoming, and in-patient treatment for excessive crying, feeding difficulties and poor weight gain are not unusual.

A proportion of the parents are obviously relieved when the diagnosis is made, but some remain resentful of what they regard as an intrusion into their privacy. It is often quite striking that those who are reticent in talking about their children are very willing to discuss their own lives and often reveal a history of deprivation in their own childhood.

THE INJURIES

1 *Head injuries*

These may be produced not only by direct trauma but also by violent acceleration or deceleration of the head. They may or may not be associated with fractures of the skull, and the absence of a fracture does not mean that the injury is any the less serious. Haemorrhage within the skull is the most important aspect of head injury, and recent attention to the 'battered baby syndrome' was heralded by the observation that children with subdural haematoma (collections of blood under a lining membrane of the brain) often had fractures of the long bones.[1]

Fractures of the skull most often involve the parietal bone, and usually only one side of the head is affected. In abused children the fractures are not infrequently multiple and irregular rather than single linear cracks.[2] A discoloured, soft swelling often appears at the site of the injury and occasionally the edge of the fractured bone may be felt. Non-accidental causes include blows to the head with heavy blunt objects and throwing children at walls or downstairs, but a number of genuine accidents can obviously produce the same effect. The correct interpretation of the cause of an injury often depends upon the history. For example, the mother of a four-month-old child with a fractured skull told me that the baby had crawled to the top of the stairs and fallen down them. A fall downstairs could have produced the injury, but babies of four months cannot crawl, and her account of the event was clearly untrue.

A type of skull fracture occasionally found in cases of non-accidental injury is of the arch of the zygoma bone just in front of the ear. This is seen when children have received a hard, swinging blow from a fist. The left side is affected most frequently because most assailants are right-handed.

Subdural haematomata may be the result of bleeding from tiny veins which pass from the cerebral cortex (brain tissue) to the venous sinuses (large blood vessels) on the surface of the brain. These may be torn when there is sudden acceleration or deceleration of the head, causing the brain to move a little within the skull. This may occur in road traffic accidents or even during fairground rides, but it can also be caused by sharp blows to the head and by violent shaking of the child. In these cases the skull may not be fractured and there may be no external sign of injury to the head. Children who have been subjected to a severe shaking by an enraged parent often have small circular bruises on the upper arms or in the middle of the back corresponding to the position of the thumbs where the child has been gripped. Another clue to non-accidental injury is that the subdural bleeding often occurs more or less symmetrically on each side of the brain.[3]

In a number of children with non-accidental head injuries there are haemorrhages into the eyes. These are recognisable by ophthalmoscopic examination and are of great significance not only in diagnosis but also because many of the affected children suffer severe visual handicap. The children do not all have detectable subdural haematomas although most of them have suffered skull fracture or major soft-tissue injuries to the head.[4-5]

2 Bone injuries

When non-accidental injury is suspected it is advisable to obtain an x-ray of the whole skeleton except for the pelvis. The latter is excluded, if possible, in order to limit exposure of the gonads to radiation and because non-accidental fractures of the pelvis are uncommon. X-ray evidence of fractures may support the diagnosis of non-accidental injury, but it is not excluded by their absence. The bone injuries are not always easily distinguishable from those occurring accidentally, but in abused children they tend to have the following characteristics: (*a*) multiplicity of fractures, (*b*) location at the growing ends of bones, (*c*) marked periosteal reaction.

(a) *Multiple fractures* are often present in widely scattered parts of the body and are sometimes associated with subdural haematoma. The injuries found are often much more extensive than would have been expected from the history or from the external signs of violence. They are frequently ascribed to falls and may be inconsistent with this and other preferred explanations. Normal children from the age of six to nine months exhibit a 'parachute reaction' on falling and put out their arms and legs to save themselves. Any fracture sustained accidentally is therefore likely to be of a greenstick type at the wrist unless the fall is from a considerable height or involves unusual forces due to leverage. In non-accidental injury the femur (thigh bone) is frequently affected, and spiral fractures through the shaft of these and other large bones are seen. It has been reported that compression fractures of the spinal vertebral bodies or fractures of their spinous processes may follow forced bending of the trunk either forwards or backwards.[6]

A characteristic feature of non-accidental injury is that fractures are not only multiple but also in different stages of repair. It is possible to give some indication of the age of a fracture from its appearance on x-ray, and old healed injuries can usually be diagnosed with confidence.

(b) *Location at the growing ends of bones.* There is a marked tendency for injuries in abused children to be at the ends of the bones, especially if the child has been handled roughly or vigorously shaken. In infancy the epiphysis (growth centre) at the end of the bone may be pulled away at the relatively weak junction of cartilage with the bone shaft. Little fragments of bone are frequently pulled off the shaft, and in addition the epiphysis may be displaced. Injuries of this type occur when there is an unreasonable pulling strain from the ends of the limbs. They may possibly be produced by swinging the baby in inappropriate play, but pain is caused and the game is unlikely to go on to cause multiple epiphyseal injuries; these are almost always due to violent punishment.

(c) *Marked periosteal reaction.* In infancy the membrane covering bone (periosteum) is not so firmly attached as in adults and may be separated as a result of bleeding underneath it or by direct trauma. The separation may not be seen on x-rays taken shortly after the injury but two or three weeks later the healing process does become visible. At this stage calcium is laid down in the injured part and further trauma during repair will result in irregularities in its outline. It is characteristic of non-accidental injury that the healing reaction in the periosteum tends to be extensive.

3 Soft-tissue injuries
These consist of scratches and other minor injuries to the surface of the skin (abrasions), capillary bleeding underneath the skin (bruises) and small tears of superficial tissues, especially in the mouth. All children get bruises and abrasions during the course of normal play, and ill treatment is inferred only if they are excessive in degree or characteristic of a particular form of punishment. Accidental soft-tissue injuries are infrequent in healthy infants under six months of age.

(a) *Abrasions.* The marks seen most often in children who have been punished are those due to the buckles of belts. Some parents consider that it is appropriate to chastise children with a strap, but none could justify assault with the buckle end of a belt or with a chain. Such punishments sometimes leave identifiable superficial injuries of the skin. Strapping with a relatively inflexible plastic belt can produce multiple cuts into the skin.

A patterned area may occur on the skin of children who receive blows at the time when they are wearing certain types of clothes such as those made of cellular cotton material.

Other easily recognised marks are the abraided lines round the ankles and wrists in children who have been tied down to their cots with string. Similar marks are made when ligatures are tied to the penis of small boys to stop them wetting. Abrasions may provide evidence of past injuries because there is often an increase in pigmentation of the affected part which remains for several weeks after the skin has healed.

(b) *Bruises* are caused by the escape of blood from tiny vessels that have ruptured under the skin. The force of the external blow or pressure required to rupture them depends upon the health of the vessel and upon the elasticity of surrounding tissues, and the latter varies in different parts of the body. So too does the extent to which blood extravasates under the skin; for example, severe trauma to the soles of the feet may produce very few marks, whereas bruising of the face can be quite extensive even after relatively minor injuries. The number of blood vessels ruptured and the amount of bleeding caused by each blow depend upon the injured part's vascularity, i.e. how many vessels there are to be broken, and this again varies in different parts of the body.

The characteristic purple colour of a fresh bruise persists for about forty-eight to seventy-two hours. Subsequently colour changes take place as a result of the breakdown of red blood corpuscles and the haemoglobin pigment which they contain. The purple colour gradually becomes brown, later turning to a pale olive green and finally pale yellow before fading after about two weeks. It is impossible to be precise about the age of a bruise because the type and vascularity of the affected tissues determine not only the extent to which the blood spreads but also the time taken for its absorption. Slight variations in colour are not, therefore, significant, but an approximate age can be stated, and the presence of fresh and fading bruises in similar parts of the body does indicate that there has been repeated trauma. Bruises can be grouped into two broad categories according to whether or not there is associated swelling of the surrounding tissue.

Blows from blunt objects tend to cause not only rupture of small blood vessels but also an extravasation of tissue fluid into adjacent parts. There is, therefore, swelling as well as bruising, and the former persists for a few days. It is the type of injury most likely to be seen after an accident — for example, when the forehead is banged against a hard object. The overlying skin may be slightly injured and show a mark consistent with the shape of an object, such as the edge of a table, against which a child has fallen. Laceration of the skin over the injured part may occur if there has been a considerable force tending to twist or tear the skin.

Of far greater significance in the diagnosis of child abuse are small, flat, circular bruises not associated with marked tissue swelling. They are commonly seen on the face of young infants and correspond to areas of pressure by the assailant's fingers. Similar marks may be found in the middle of the back on each side of the spine in young infants and over the front of the upper arms in older children who have been severely shaken. On the face there are commonly three or four bruises on the left cheek or jaw to every one on the right cheek, and they are caused by frantic efforts to stop the baby crying or to force him to retain food. There may be several crops of fingertip bruises of different ages, and their recognition can be vitally important because injuries of this type are sometimes the prelude to sreious battering. Fingertip bruising of the trunk due to karate-type prodding blows has been recorded.[7]

Characteristic marks are produced by pinches and bites. The former consist of slightly curved parallel bruises, usually on the limbs and sometimes showing superficial scratches from fingernails. Bites cause two hemispherical marks, and the position of the teeth may be outlined by injuries to the skin. The marks caused by teeth can be matched to dental impressions of suspected assailants and are of considerable forensic importance. In addition, salivary antibodies can be detected in samples taken from the unwashed skin of children thought to have suffered bites.

(c) *Injuries to the mouth.* In cases of child abuse there is a predilection for trauma to the face and especially around the mouth. Occasionally the frenulum of the upper lip (i.e. the skin fold from the inside of the lip to the gum margin) is torn when the lip is pushed forcibly upwards. This can happen when a feeding bottle is pushed into the mouth impatiently.

4 *Burns*

Burns can be inflicted upon children in several different ways. Those of the mouth can be sustained not only by feeds that are too hot but also from administered corrosive poison. Small burns, particularly at the angles of the mouth, may be seen when very hot milk has been offered and quickly rejected by the child.

Punishment of children by sitting them on cooker hotplates or by holding them over fires occurs occasionally and causes fairly extensive, though usually superficial, burns to the buttocks. A similar but more damaging form of abuse is that perpetrated by parents who hold their child's hand to the bar of an electric fire. In two cases known to me both the mothers were of low intelligence.

Injuries that have been mentioned frequently in the past decade are those due to cigarette burns. Stubbing of cigarettes on the skin causes small circular burns of variable depth and if present they are usually found on the hands, thighs or buttocks and are often multiple. The amount of scarring left after the burn has healed depends on its depth and the degree of secondary infection.

5 Injuries of the abdomen and chest

These are less common than the head injuries, fractures and bruises previously described and they may present considerable diagnostic problems. The need for urgent treatment is likely to overshadow other considerations, and the possibility of non-accidental injury may not be suspected at first. Fist blows to the abdomen do not produce significant external marks, and the nature of injuries to abdominal organs may not be recognised prior to operative surgical treatment.

The most common injury is rupture of the small intestines. This requires a lot of force because the intestines are mobile structures and they readily squelch out of the way on impact except at points of attachment in the epigastrium (upper abdomen) and the right iliac fossa (just above the right groin). Perforation of the stomach or urinary bladder may occur, and tears of the liver and spleen can be produced. The latter will result in substantial internal bleeding. All these injuries cause shock and collapse and demand urgent life-saving treatment.

Haemorrhage may occur into the wall of the intestine or behind the peritoneum (lining of the abdominal cavity). Blows to the small of the back may injure the kidneys and cause bleeding which may either be obvious or require microscopic examination of the urine for its detection.

Fractures of the ribs are common in abused children but injury to underlying structure is unusual. Nevertheless, the lung is occasionally lacerated, causing it to collapse, and haemorrhage within the chest may occur. Non-accidental damage to almost every organ in the body, including the heart, has been recorded.

DIFFERENTIAL DIAGNOSIS

In order to avoid inappropriate action in cases of suspected non-accidental injury it is very important that all alternative diagnoses should be considered. It would compound the tragedy of illness if the parents of a sick child were to be falsely accused of causing his injuries.

Subdural haematoma can be the result of relatively minor accidental trauma as well as of acceleration and deceleration of the head in a variety of circumstances. It may be a late manifestation of birth injury, especially if the baby was premature or the confinement difficult. Other possible causes are some types of meningitis, which can leave residual collections of blood in the subdural space.

The only injuries in abused children that are rarely, if ever, simulated by disease processes are those in which the epiphyses are displaced and small fragments of bone pulled away from their growing ends. Nevertheless, even these injuries may be seen in very young infants following difficult confinements, especially in those delivered by breech. Over-zealous physiotherapy in children with diminished sensation in their limbs may produce the same effect.

Multiple fractures can be found not only in children who are non-accidentally injured but also in those who have certain bone abnormalities. The most important of these is osteogenesis imperfecta (fragile bone disease), in which the bone matrix fails to form properly. Affected children have thin bones with a variable degree of fragility. They have a noticeable joint laxity and tend to have small, deformed teeth. The sclera of the eye, normally white, is very thin and has a bluish colour. This disease tends to run in families and there is sometimes an associated family history of deafness. Multiple fractures may be the result of brittleness of the bones, and this occurs in another disease called osteopetrosis. In this condition the bone architecture is abnormal and it lacks the strength of normal bone. Thin, poorly mineralised bone is a feature of several other diseases, such as rickets and hypophosphatasia, in which there is an increased propensity for them to fracture. Finally, the possibility of stress fractures and of fractures at the site of the bone cysts and of secondary deposits from leukaemia and other malignant conditions have to be considered.

Bruises and painful haemorrhages under the periosteum giving a radiological appearance like that in an abused child may occur in scurvy owing to lack of vitamin C. Similar x-ray findings which have to be distinguished from those of injury are caused by inflammation of the periosteum, which is a feature of some cases of congenital syphilis. Subperiosteal new bone formation without irregularity of the shaft of the bone may also be seen in a disease called infantile cortical hyperostosis, and this may occasionally simulate healed traumatic injury.

Multiple scars due to tearing of the skin are found in an inherited disease called the Ehlers–Danlos syndrome. There is a lack of normal elasticity in the skin, and although the marks may look a little like those of inflicted injury the tendency to the condition is usually well known in affected families.

Bruising presents a difficult problem, because several diseases can lead to an increased liability to bleed. In all cases in which the diagnosis of non-accidental injury depends on the presence of bruises, tests for coagulation defects should be done. Absence from the blood of factors responsible for normal clotting will lead to more frequent and extensive bruising than would otherwise occur with trivial injuries. Some of the diseases, such as haemophilia, have an inherited basis. Others, such as scurvy, are due to vitamin deficiency, while for some, such as idiopathic thrombocytopoenia, the cause is unknown. Bruising may also be a manifestation of malignant disease such as leukaemia. In children with bleeding disorders a pattern of bruising similar to that in abused children is unusual.

Self-inflicted trauma may occur in children with a rare disability in which they do not have normal perception of pain. This is a serious handicap because they can sustain serious injuries as a result of uninhibited play. In a child known to me, who had successive fractures and a ruptured bladder, the diagnosis of non-accidental injury was suspected until his true problem was understood.

CONCLUSION AND SUMMARY

A very wide range of conditions may be produced by parents who actively abuse their children. Some are life-threatening but others do not in themselves cause serious or permanent damage. The latter are nevertheless important because repetition of violence is frequent and in subsequent episodes the child may lose his life or become severely handicapped.

Medical skills are usually necessary in defining the nature and extent of trauma, but the assertion that injuries are non-accidental is rarely susceptible to scientific proof. In a few cases the techniques of forensic pathology are helpful but in the majority diagnosis rests upon an opinion. The reliability of the opinion may vary, therefore, not only with the nature of the injuries but also with the experience of the examiner. Conclusions about the probable cause of injuries often depend a great deal upon whether they are consistent with the history and the child's stage of development.

Non-accidental injury is particularly associated with certain types of traumatic condition. These include subdural haematoma together with multiple fractures of the long bones, intraocular haemorrhages, trauma to the growing ends of bones and injuries with subsequent marked periosteal reaction. Abrasions may delineate the nature of trauma, and fingertip bruising, especially on an infant's face, is strongly suggestive of abuse. Bite marks and some burns are fairly readily distinguishable from accidents, but damage to the abdominal or thoracic viscera may present difficult diagnostic problems.

There is a grave danger that the heightened awareness of child abuse and the recent severe public criticism of failure to protect children may lead to over-diagnosis. A considerable number of diseases can simulate non-accidental injury and lead to a wrong diagnosis. Great care has to be taken to avoid this, not only because it may lead to an injustice but also because it may jeopardise the parent–child relationship and the professional integrity of the diagnostician. Caution should never be allowed to endanger the child's life, but action should be taken only after the fullest consideration of all the circumstances.

REFERENCES

[1] Caffey, J. (1946), *Am. J. Roentgenol. Radium Therapy. Nucl. Med.,* 56, 163.
[2] Silverman, F. N. (1974), in *The battered child,* ed, R. E. Helfer and C. H. Kempe. Second edition, University of Chicago Press.
[3] Guthkelch, N. (1971), *Brit. Med. J.,* i, 430.
[4] Harcourt, B., and Hopkins, D. (1971), *Brit. Med. J.,* ii, 398.
[5] Mushin, A. S. (1971), *Brit. Med. J.,* ii, 402.
[6] Swischuk, L. E. (1969), *Radiology, 92,* 733.
[7] Hall, M. H. (1974), *The Police Surgeon, 6,* 17.

John Pickett   *NSPCC regional social work manager*

4 THE MANAGEMENT OF NON-ACCIDENTAL INJURY TO CHILDREN IN THE CITY OF MANCHESTER

Cases of *repeated* non-accidental injury, causing death or permanent disability, are usually characterised by serious deficiencies in professional judgement or service.[1] These cases demonstrate that ability to help effectively is constrained not only by limited knowledge but also by limited use of available knowledge and resources through failures in communication. It should be possible to reduce the number of such tragedies by the use of multidisciplinary therapeutic teams working in close communication and co-operation. If such teams are to be brought together, major problems which impede collaboration will need to be overcome.[2] Goodwill and mutual trust will be necessary to reconcile the disparate obligations and duties to heal, protect and control which are contained within the professions involved. Area Review Committees[3] could become the enabling agents which provide the opportunity and challenge of interprofessional collaboration in the treatment of non-accidental injury to children.

A system of notification, intervention, co-ordination and review has been developed in Manchester which may provide a useful model for others to adopt. The system is based on the assumption that effective communication and co-ordination can occur only where responsibility for their existence and maintenance is clearly defined and vested in individuals who have the kind of specialised knowledge which enables them to work across the boundaries of the professions involved, who also have a clear sense of commitment to their task, and who have authority to carry it out. These attributes can exist only within a multidisciplinary team.

The Manchester scheme began to evolve in 1970, when a multidisciplinary committee was established under the chairmanship of John Davis, Professor of Child Health at Manchester University. In its early days the committee's work was confined to cases of non-accidental injury occurring to children under four years of age. Since January 1975 its work has extended to include all non-accidentally injured children under sixteen years. The committee is known as the Manchester Child Abuse Policy Committee.

In 1971—72 the committee considered how it might increase effectiveness in the management of cases, and recognised the need for a specialist team to supplement and strengthen existing services. Following detailed discussions,[4] the Social Services Department and the National Society for the Prevention of Cruelty to Children jointly funded and set up a special unit staffed by NSPCC social work specialists in child abuse and supported by consultants in paediatrics and psychiatry, with the Child Abuse Policy Committee acting as an advisory body.[5] The unit became operational in January 1973, and its main *functions* are:

1 To provide social work services for families referred where non-accidental injury is known or thought to have occurred.
2 To provide opportunities for consultation and discussion of such cases held by other social workers, health and medical personnel, with the aim of promoting good practice.
3 To maintain a central case register of all suspected cases of non-accidental injury to children under sixteen years of age.
4 To co-ordinate services within the city of Manchester, ensuring that case conferences are held, where appropriate. All notified cases are periodically reviewed, and good communication is maintained between the professions involved.
5 To undertake research into the problem.
6 To provide information to the professions and general public about the nature and extent of the problem.

ORGANISATION

The unit is staffed by a team leader, five team members and a unit co-ordinator. This team is responsible for the case work and consultative services, the maintenance of the case register, and the co-ordination of services within the city of Manchester. Paediatric and psychiatric consultants are available to aid diagnosis and treatment. The case-work service is confined to families residing within the city. All cases referred have to satisfy the following criteria:

1 The child is under the age of sixteen years, and normally cared for by at least one legal parent.
2 The child has an injury, and is thought to be at risk of further injury.
3 The nature of the injury is not consistent with the parents' or caretaker's account of how it occurred, or other factors indicate that it was probably caused non-accidentally.
4 The family resides within the prescribed catchment area.

The unit team is on call twenty-four hours a day, using radio paging equipment to achieve total availability. Limited case loads of approximately twelve per worker are carried. Co-workers are used in most cases to minimise over-dependence on individual workers. All case-work staff are 'authorised persons' empowered to remove children and institute care proceedings. The unit staff will also institute criminal proceedings when necessary.

The primary focus of social work treatment is the preservation of the life and health of the child, preferably within its natural home surroundings. In some cases this would be an unrealistic aim and a healthy severance of the parent–child relationship has to be attempted.

In an attempt to meet the unmet dependency needs which seem to characterise most abusing parents, a supportive 'on demand' service is offered, with frequent contact and home visiting as part of the reaching-out process. Extensive use is made of day nursery care, and nursery staff play a crucial role in therapy. Group therapy is provided for parents, and voluntary workers are used as 'family friends' to extend and supplement case-work help.

The consultation service. Because of the limited number of cases the unit can service by direct case work, and the need to spread knowledge and ability to manage other cases of suspected non-accidental injury through the health and social services, a consultation service is seen as an integral part of the unit's functions. This service is available to staff from hospitals, departments of health and social services, voluntary agencies and the police, and seeks to promote the development of informed attitudes towards child abuse, and adequate communication across the disciplines involved. The service is available to personnel within the Greater Manchester metropolitan county, but because of the very heavy demands on the service priority is given to all cases occurring within the city of Manchester and those occurring elsewhere within the catchment area which present special difficulties to the personnel involved. There are three main areas for consultation, namely diagnosis, treatment planning, and management procedures.

Some cases present no difficulty in medical/social diagnosis, but the majority are much less clear-cut. No firm diagnosis is possible and treatment has to proceed on the basis of a suspected non-accidental injury. Confronted with the problem of diagnosis, social work and medical personnel are naturally concerned that they should not wrongly accuse a parent of battering his or her child. This proper concern can, however, lead to failure to diagnose in the absence of adequate consultation. The diagnosis of non-accidental injury is a medico-social diagnosis, and should always involve at least a doctor and a social worker in consultation together, but will often need to involve much wider multidisciplinary consideration, probably at a case conference. Unit staff undertake many individual consultations or accept invitations to attend case conferences at the diagnostic stage of management. It is at this early, crucial stage that many far-reaching decisions will have to be made about the future management of the case. Social workers are encouraged to consult the team on all aspects of case-work management.

Consultations usually centre round social management planning, with particular emphasis on a prognostic evaluation and the overall focus of social management, including the use of medical and psychiatric consultation, and of community resources. Clarification is often sought in decision-making about care proceedings, the removal of a child or return home, and the transfer and closing of cases. Help is often sought in interpreting and responding to recurrent minor injury during the life span of a case. Consultations usually occur with individual medical or social work practitioners, or at case conferences. Records are kept of all consultations, and mutually agreed with the personnel involved.

Unit staff are members of all the Area Review Committees within the Greater Manchester metropolitan county, and assist in the evaluation of existing arrangements, agency policies and resources. Arrangements for the management of cases differ according to local needs and practices. The unit carries information about the management procedures laid down by each Area Review Committee within the metropolitan county, and this information is available to social work and medical practitioners.

The central case register. In contrast to practice in the United States, no one in Britain is required by law to notify cases of child abuse to the protective services, and very little support appears to exist for the introduction of reporting laws. There is, however, a growing body of opinion supporting the view that voluntary registers should form an integral part of management procedures for child abuse.

In 1970 the Standing Medical Advisory Committee[6] stressed the importance of co-ordination of information, pointing out that cases can appear in different departments of the same hospital, or different hospitals in the same area, and that a wide range of medical and social work personnel are likely to encounter the problem in their work. The committee suggested that if registers were set up information could be more readily available to medical staff to aid medical diagnoses, and to *ensure that effective preventive measures are taken.* This point is of great importance — that registers should be not merely an aid to diagnosis but a resource point from which action will be initiated. The value of registration has also been stressed by the NSPCC and the Department of Health and Social Security.[7]

William Ireland[8] considers the main value of registers to be: identification of multiple abuse within the same family, education of the public about the nature and extent of the problem, the provision of a basis for further definition of the phenomenon, and the development of an intervention and treatment programme. Many of the systems of registration in America combine the functions of case identification, provision of service and the collection and dissemination of information through research programmes. These functions precisely mirror the needs which are apparent in Britain and can be met through an effective registration system linked to service delivery.

Registration can succeed only in an atmosphere of trust and full participation between all the professions involved, e.g. doctors, social workers, health visitors, teachers, police, etc. This requires a major shift of attitude on the part of the professions in relation to the question of confidentiality. Just as there is no legal obligation to report suspected non-accidental injury, neither, it appears, is there legal remedy against persons acting in good faith who do so.[9] Nevertheless concern is felt not only about the legality of sharing information, but also with professional ethics. Professional confidentiality, however, cannot be and is not absolute, and when the best interests of the child are served by sharing information in order to secure essential medical—social treatment there should be no ethical conflict. Non-accidental injury is a medical—social disease, requiring medical and social treatment, and the patient/client is a child with rights of cure. In notifying cases of suspected non-accidental injury to a register the professions are protecting the rights of the child, not violating them. We must also ask, 'Who is ill?' Abused children do not exist in healthy families, and for each abused child there will be parents desperately in need of help.

The register maintained by the special unit covers the Greater Manchester metropolitan county, a conurbation of ten metropolitan districts, populated by 2.7 million people, including 711,492 children under sixteen years.[10] Mobility results in families moving into a succession of different local authority areas, and being treated in any of the twenty-two hospitals with children's wards. The central register provides a central point of reference as an aid to diagnosis, is immediately accessible 'round the clock', and is linked to a team of child abuse experts who are available for consultation and who work within a child-protective service which has the capacity to respond immediately in bringing help to the child and family. Access to information held on the register is limited to doctors and senior designated personnel within health and social service agencies as defined by the Area Review Committees. A 'ring back' procedure is used to check authenticity.

Each Area Review Committee has established a local register which is linked to the central register, using a common criterion for inclusion on the register, which is: 'All physically injured children under the age of sixteen years[11] where the nature of the injury is not consistent with the account of how it occurred, or where other factors indicate that there is reasonable suspicion that the injury was inflicted or not prevented by any person having custody, charge or care of the child'. Register information is compiled by the unit co-ordinator through comprehensive contacts with the notifying agencies. The information is recorded on a standard form and a detailed cross-index system (see appendixes 4.1–2). Register information includes the age, sex and ordinal position of the referred child, household composition and family structure, information on housing size, type of tenure and amenity lack; the obstetric history of the referred child, the process of referral to the register, details of the notified injuries, previous and subsequent injuries; cultural and stress factors. A clinical judgement is recorded on each set of injuries as to their severity and the likelihood of their having been sustained non-accidentally, using index of suspicion and severity rating scales (see appendix 4.2).

The NSPCC is undertaking research into data held on the registers of its special units.[12] Data will be examined in relation to existing local and national census and medical statistics in order to establish the extent to which characteristics of the sub-population in which child abuse is known or suspected to have occurred differ from those of the general population, in so far as this is possible, having regard to variable notification response. Confidentiality is preserved by numeric coding within the units, transferred to cards, and stored on magnetic tape, with updating provision.

In addition to providing comprehensive recorded information the register is designed to provide detailed and up-to-date statistical information which is required by Area Review Committees, NSPCC special units, local authority departments, and others involved in this field. This information is likely to be of value in:

1   Estimating and planning for suitable provision for non-accidentally injured children and their families on the basis of reported injury.

2   Identifying areas of apparent under-reporting, or weaknesses in the existing

structure for dealing with the problem of non-accidental injury.

3   Relating differential rates of reported incidence to specific social and environmental features of a given area.[12]

Co-ordination in Manchester. The case register maintained by the special unit is in essence a depository of information from all sources, to which all designated personnel can relate as a first step in diagnosis and treatment. Its effectiveness is largely dependent upon the extent to which it is used and understood by the senior designated personnel responsible for field staff, and by the medical profession. Once notified, the case is brought to the attention of the special unit team, to which the Child Abuse Policy Committee delegates authority and responsibility to initiate appropriate action to protect the child and bring help to the family.

Members of the Child Abuse Policy Committee have collaborated to produce procedural guidelines in the form of a nineteen-page booklet giving detailed advice on the steps to be taken once non-accidental injury is suspected. Ten thousand copies of these guidelines have been distributed in conjunction with a pamphlet on non-accidental injury which is designed as an aid to the identification of suspected cases (see appendixes 4.3—4). The procedural guidelines are specifically designed to take account of the interrelated functions of the personnel involved, and to guide personnel into channels of communication both interdepartmentally and inter-professionally. Special emphasis has been given to delineating the role of senior designated staff members in advising and supporting field staff. Provision is also made for specialist social work and paediatric consultation to be available.

Once a case is notified to the special unit, steps are immediately taken to check that communication is occurring between those involved. A decision is reached as to whether a case conference is necessary; in most cases it is. Unit staff are responsible for ensuring that the case conference is held, and that all appropriate personnel are invited. A unit staff member attends, acting as consultant to the conference, and representing the Child Abuse Policy Committee. In addition, both major children's hospitals in the city have co-ordinating paediatricians who are available to attend case conferences or provide a further opinion or advice to other medical consultants. The unit's consultant paediatrician and psychiatrist are also available for consultation and referral.

The case conference is designed to bring together all those who can provide information about the child and his family or who have responsibility for the health and safety of the child, and for providing services. This, of course, includes the police, who share the general concern to avoid unilateral action. It is recognised that each agency must retain the right to act independently in accordance with its own policies, but every effort is made to reach mutually agreed decisions; so far there have not been any instances of unilateral action by any participants. The primary function of the case conference is to make an assessment, formulate a plan of action, and decide who shall accept primary responsibility for the social management of the case.

A well ordered and efficient case conferencing system is no guarantee against failures in communication; at its best it merely ensures that, at a given point in time, adequate communication is occurring. Good case management requires a high level of therapeutic skill and effective communication and co-ordination throughout the life span of the case. Most cases are managed, however, against a background of inadequate record-keeping, faulty communications and seemingly endless changes in the personnel involved. For these reasons a process of constant monitoring seems essential.

Monitoring. Although cases can be monitored within an agency, if we accept the premise that they require multidisciplinary management, then case monitoring should at the very least involve two agencies. Similarly, if we ask for the same information from two people who are supposed to be in close communication we should be able to judge the effectiveness of that communication by the extent to which their answers are congruent.

A monitoring service has been instituted for all notified cases in Manchester, and is operated by the special unit. At three-monthly intervals monitor forms (see appendix 4.5) are sent to the Community Physician (Child Health) and the head of the social work agency servicing the family, and are passed on and returned through these senior personnel back to the unit. This procedure ensures that the senior personnel responsible for field staff are able to assess the case from their point of view before returning the monitor forms to the special unit.

The monitoring service is designed to test whether communication is occurring between two of the key agencies involved, assess the status of the case, and make judgements about whether any additional action is required, initiating that action, and updating the data on the register record. Cases are withdrawn from the monitoring service only when both agencies have agreed on four separate occasions that the child is no longer at risk.

In order to make these judgements a series of questions are asked which are designed to highlight circumstantial changes, renewed injury to the child, injury to other children in the family, gaps in information, or information known to one agency and not the other, and so on. An examination of the circumstantial changes that are occurring will often provide important clues about the extent to which the family may be experiencing increased stress, or improvements in its circumstances.

When the forms are returned to the special unit a comparative scrutiny is undertaken for inconsistencies, communication failure or factors indicating increasing stress or risk to the child or siblings. Immediate consultation occurs with the respondents, and further action is initiated if necessary.

At first it was thought that field staff might view the monitoring service as an intrusion and a threat to their professional status, but this does not appear to be the case. Busy field staff, faced with excessive demands on their time and resources, seem to welcome the discipline and support involved in a periodic review of some of their most worrying cases.

Difficulties arise in trying to assess the effectiveness of the procedures I have described. When sufficient data have been collected, it will be possible to demonstrate the incidence of reported non-accidental injury within a given population, the rate of recurring injury before as well as after notification, and morbidity and mortality rates, and to make comparisons with existing data in so far as that is possible, given the different nature of the samples involved. These factors will, however, provide only a crude index from which to make inferences about the efficacy of the procedures. Judgements about the quality of the care provided for the non-accidentally injured child and its family, and the extent to which this influences its physical and emotional well-being, would require major resources for research.

The system of management I have described relates only to children who have suffered suspected non-accidental injury, but this is only part of the larger problem of child abuse, which must include parental neglect, both physical and emotional, and ill treatment of children. Child abuse must surely also include the more noxious influences of our culture, from which we recoil, but which we nevertheless bequeath to our children. It is a natural human reaction to partialise a problem too large to contemplate, but it should not lead us to false assumptions. Perhaps if we can learn how to reach and help this group of children and their parents we shall be a step nearer to grasping the totality of the problem.

ACKNOWLEDGEMENTS

The special unit staff are indebted to all their professional colleagues in Manchester for their help in establishing and maintaining the system of co-ordination described. All the professions involved are especially indebted to the Manchester Social Services Committee. It is their support, allied to that of the NSPCC, which made the project possible.

NOTES

1   Skinner A. E., and Castle, R. L., *Seventy-eight battered children: a retrospective study*, Battered Child Research Department, NSPCC, 1969; *Inquiry into the circumstances surrounding the death of Graham Bagnall and the role of the County Council's social services*, Salop County Council, 1973; *Report of the Committee of Inquiry into the care and supervision provided in relation to Maria Colwell*, Department of Health and Social Security, HMSO, 1974; *Report* of the committee of inquiry into the case of Richard Clark; Graeme Bowd, 'I now confess I did kill my baby son', *Daily Mail*, 3 September 1974.
2   Carter, J., 'Co-ordination and planning of services', in *The Maltreated Child*, ed. J. Carter, Priory Press, London, 1974.
3   DHSS, *Non-accidental injury to children*, LASSL (74) 13, CMD (74) 8, HMSO, 1974.
4   Owtram, P. J., 'NSPCC special units', *Social Work Service*, No. 8, December 1975.
5   The Manchester unit was the first of a number of special units established by the NSPCC.
6   'The battered baby', Standing Medical Advisory Committee memorandum, DHSS, 1970.
7   Castle, R. L., and Kerr, A. M., *A study of suspected child abuse*, NSPCC, 1972; DHSS, *Non-accidental Injury to Children*, LASSL (74) 13, CMD (74) 8, HMSO, 1974.
8   Ireland, W. H., 'A registry on child abuse', *Children*, 13, May–June 1966, pp. 113–15.
9   Medical Defence Union, *Annual Report*, 1974.
10 *Registrar General's Census of England and Wales, 1971*, HMSO, 1973.
11 One metropolitan district includes all children up to the age of seventeen years.
12 'Registers of suspected non-accidental injury: a report on registers maintained in Leeds and Manchester by NSPCC special units', NSPCC, January 1976.
13 Gregg, Grace, 'Physician, child abuse reporting laws, and injured child: psycho-social anatomy of childhood trauma', *Clinical Paediatrics*, vol. 7, 721, 1968.

Appendixes 4.1–5. It should be noted that some of the forms have since been modified in the light of experience.

APPENDIX 4.1

The original is in the form of a foolscap folder with a pocket for documents.

SURNAME: **REGISTER OF SUSPECTED NON-ACCIDENTAL INJURY TO CHILDREN**   **INDEX NUMBER:**

NSPCC SPECIAL UNIT (   )

FORENAMES:	Alias:	d.o.b.	M/F

HOME ADDRESS: (1)

(2)

(3)

REGISTERED BY: Name: Agency: Date:

RESIDENT PARENTS OR CARETAKERS (at time of registration)   OTHERS RESIDENT IN HOUSEHOLD (name, relationship, significant information)

FEMALE   UM   M   S   D   W   C   Natural/Other: (1)

Name   d.o.b.   CR

Nee/Alias   c.o.b.   (2)

Occupation   CR

Criminal Record   CR   (3)   CR

MALE   UM   M   S   D   W   C   Natural/Other: PAST CARETAKERS, OTHER SIGNIFICANT PERSONS (name, relationship, significant information)

Name   d.o.b   (1)

Alias   c.o.b.   CR

Occupation   (2)

Criminal Record   CR   CR

CARETAKING CHANGES SINCE REFERRAL (date, details, relevant monitor)   (3)

    CR

    CR

STATUTORY OR VOLUNTARY CARE PROCESS

date	type	agency	present status

CHILDREN (state relationship if not natural, and if non-resident or deceased)

(1)	d.o.b.	M/F CR		
(2)	d.o.b.	M/F CR		
(3)	d.o.b.	M/F CR		
(4)	d.o.b.	M/F CR		
(5)	d.o.b.	M/F CR		
(6)	d.o.b.	M/F CR		

MONITORED (date)

(1)	(2)	(3)
(4)	(5)	(6)	(7)
(8)	(9)	(10)	(11)

71

SOCIAL AND MEDICAL AGENCIES INVOLVED

S.W.(1)	From:	Hospital (1)	From:
Tel:	To:	Tel:	To:
Agency:		Consultant:	
S.W.(2)	From:	Hospital (2)	From:
Tel:	To:	Tel:	To:
Agency:		Consultant:	
S.W.(3)	From:	Hospital (3)	From:
Tel:	To:	Tel:	To:
Agency:		Consultant:	
S.W.(4)	From:	G.P. (1)	From:
Tel:	To:	Tel:	To:
Agency:		G.P. (2)	From:
S.W.(5)	From:	Tel:	To:
Tel:	To:	G.P. (3)	From:
Agency:		Tel:	To:
S.W.(6)	From:	M.C.W. Clinic (1)	From:
Tel:	To:	Tel:	To:
Agency:		M.C.W. Clinic (2)	From:
School/Preschool (1)	From:	Tel:	To:
	To:	M.C.W. Clinic (3)	From:
School/Preschool (2)	From:	Tel:	To:
	To:	H.V. (1)	From:
School/Preschool (3)	From:	Tel:	To:
	To:	H.V. (2)	From:
OTHER PERSONS INVOLVED		Tel:	To:
		H.V. (3)	From:
		Tel:	To:
		OTHER MEDICAL AGENCIES	

REFERRAL HISTORY (Trace action initiated following injury, including action by parents if any)

Referred by _____ To _____ Date _____

Referred by _____ To _____ Date _____

Referred by _____ To _____ Date _____

OBSTETRIC HISTORY

FT/P

Birth Weight:

Place of birth: Home/Hospital:

Birth abnormalities:

MEDICAL HISTORY

Failure to thrive:

ACCOMMODATION (at time of registration)

Number of rooms: Time in residence:

Type: House/Flat (Storey:)/Rooms/Other:

Tenure: O.Occ./Council/Rented U-F/Rented F/Other:

Amenities: Cooker: E S L   Bath: E S L   Hot water: E S L   Kitchen sink: E S L

Inside W.C.: E S L   Outside W.C.: E S L

Date moved: see monitor:

FINANCE (at time of registration)

Approximate nett weekly income:

Supplementary benefit: Yes/No

Date position changed: see monitor:

CULTURAL FACTORS

STRESS FACTORS

ANY OTHER DETAILS

HISTORY OF INJURIES

Index of Suspicion Rating 1-5
Index of Severity Rating A-D

Date	Details of each set of injuries, with explanation if given		Treated by	Action
	PREVIOUS INJURIES			
	NOTIFIED INJURIES			
	SUBSEQUENT INJURIES			

APPENDIX 4.2

Special unit (Manchester)
5 Wynnstay Grove
Fallowfield, Manchester M14 6XG

061-248 6060 (office hours), 061-832 6677 (after-hours emergency)

GUIDE TO COMPLETION OF REGISTER RECORD FOR
NSPCC SPECIAL UNIT
REGISTER OF SUSPECTED NON-ACCIDENTAL INJURY TO CHILDREN

I. *Criteria for registration*
All cases of suspected non-accidental injury, notified to the unit for whatever
reason, must be placed on the case register if the following criteria are satisfied:

1 The child must not be more than sixteen years old on the date of registration.
2 The child must normally reside in the Greater Manchester Metropolitan County.
3(a) *If the child has an injury* the following criteria should apply: All physically
injured children under the age of sixteen years where the nature of the injury is not
consistent with the account of how it occurred or where other factors indicate that
there is a reasonable suspicion that the injury was inflicted or not prevented by any
person having custody, charge or care of the child.
(b) *If the child is not physically injured,* but is considered by the notifier to be at
risk of injury, registration should take place.

II. *Procedure*
As much information as is practicable should be obtained from the notifying agent
at the time of notification, and entered on the register file. The file should then be
passed to the unit secretary/co-ordinator, who will seek missing information and
ensure that all appropriate documentation has been completed.

III. *Information*
Index number. Every child on the register should be given an individual index
number. The first two figures of this number identify the unit concerned; the
remaining figures identify the individual child. Numbers are assigned to each child
in sequence. This number should be used in any documentation which relates to
this child.
Surname. Enter the surname used by the child, in its usual spelling.
Forenames. Enter the child's forenames in full.
Alias. Enter here any other names by which the child or family is known.
D.o.b. Enter the exact date of birth of the child.
M/F. Indicate the sex of the child by ringing M (male) or F (female).
Address. Enter under (1) the child's home address at the time of registration. Any
changes in address should be entered under (2) or (3) as soon as they come to notice.
Registered by. Enter here the name and agency of the notifying agent, and the date
on which the first notification was received.
Resident parents or caretakers. This section refers to the child's resident parents, or

those acting in that capacity, at the time of registration.

    i The relationship, and marital status, of resident parents or caretakers are indicated by ringing as many of the following key letters as apply: UM — unmarried; M — married; S — separated; D — divorced; W — widowed; C — cohabiting.

    ii The relationship of the person concerned to the subject child is indicated by ringing 'Natural', in the case of the biological parent, or by specifying the relationship precisely under 'Other', e.g. stepfather, foster mother, uncle, etc.

    iii *Name.* Enter the full name of the person here.

    iv *D.o.b.* If the precise date of birth is not known, the approximate age of the person concerned at the time of registration should be entered.

    v *Née/Alias.* Give here the maiden name of the mother, if appropriate, and any other names by which the person concerned is known.

    vi *C.o.b.* Enter the country of birth of the person concerned, if it is not Great Britain.

    vii *Occupation.* Give as precise details of employment as possible. If not employed, give approximate length of unemployment, and nature of last employment if known. Any changes in this information should be entered as soon as they emerge.

    viii *Criminal record.* Give date and brief details of any known convictions. Note any subsequent convictions as soon as they come to light.

Caretaking changes since registration. Enter here details of any changes in the resident parents or caretakers of the subject child since the initial registration. Give the date, and the reference number of any relevant monitor.

Children. List here all children living in the household in birth order, eldest first, including the subject child (*who should be underlined*). Give details of the interrelationships involved if other children are not natural siblings of the subject child (e.g. child of first husband, adopted child, etc). Give date of birth (if not known give approximate age at registration), and indicate sex by circling M or F. If more than six children live in the household, note additional children in the extra space provided.

Others resident in household. List here, by name, other adults living in the household, their relationship to the subject child or parents, and any other significant information.

Past caretakers, other significant persons. List here, by name, anyone known to have had care or custody of the child in the past, or any other adults who play a significant part in the household (e.g. grandparents). Indicate their relationship to the subject child or parents and other significant information.

Cross-reference

A check should be made for previous notifications involving any individual named on the register. If a notification involving any individual is discovered, the appropriate index number should be entered under CR (cross-reference), on each document. The names of all individuals noted on the register file should be placed in the cross-index at the time of registration.

Statutory or voluntary care process. Enter here the date and type of any voluntary care or statutory care or supervision order, or any other court order which relates to this child, together with the responsible agency. Under 'Present status' note whether the order is still in force at the time of registration, or the date when it ceased to be operative. Enter any changes in this information as soon as they come to light.

Monitored. Enter here the date of each occasion when the child is monitored.
History of injuries. Give details of notified injuries, and details of any previous injuries. For each set of injuries, state by whom the injury was treated, and the action taken (e.g. admitted to hospital, out-patient treatment, GP treatment, etc). *Wherever possible, the parents' explanation of the injury should be noted.*

All injuries should be entered, however minor, and regardless of whether they are thought to be accidental or non-accidental. Details of failure to thrive, unexplained convulsions, etc, should be included.

Each set of injuries should be rated on two scales, the rating representing a socio-clinical judgement in the light of all available evidence.

Index of suspicion. The following five-point scale should be used:

1 Certain
  i All cases where one or other parent or guardian admits to having inflicted trauma.
  ii All proven court cases. (This may require altering a rating following a court case. Where a court case is pending when a notification is made, the rating can await the outcome of the case.)
2 Very suspicious
  All cases where one of Gregg's factors apply:
  i Where there is a history of accident, do the details of that accident adequately explain the location and extent of the injuries?
  ii If the child is supposed to have contributed to the accident through its own motor activity, is the alleged activity consistent with his developmental level?
  iii Are there significant discrepancies in the story of the accident as reported by various responsible adults?
  iv Where there is more than one injury, and where these have occurred at distinctly different times, can each be adequately explained?
  v Or in any case where there are unexplained injuries.
3 Suspicious
  i All cases where the injury could conceivably have been caused in the manner described but where the history and/or circumstances of the family indicate a high level of risk, e.g. history of serious deprivation, the presence of chronic or acute stress, previous history of suspicious injury, etc.
  ii Where there is inadequately explained ingestion of toxic substance.
4 Accidental
  Injuries medically confirmed as accidental, or witnessed as accidental by a reliable observer.
5 Prodromal
  All cases referred to the register because it is thought that non-accidental injury may occur.

Index of severity. The following four-point scale should be used:

A Fatal
  All cases resulting in death, where the cause of death is medically confirmed to be due to non-accidental injury.
B Serious
  All fractures, head injuries, internal injuries, severe burns, ingestion of toxic substances.

C Moderate
    All soft-tissue injuries of a superficial nature.
D Prodromal
    Where no injuries are present.

Social and medical agencies involved. Enter here the name, agency, address and telephone number of each social worker, doctor, health visitor, hospital, school or pre-school involved with this child and family at the time of registration, together with the approximate date of their first involvement. Any changes in personnel involved should be entered as soon as they come to notice.

Referral history. Trace here, as precisely as possible, the action initiated by all individuals concerned (including the child's parents) following the notified injury up to the time of registration.

Obstetric history. Note here the birth-weight of the child, the place of birth, and whether the birth was full-term (FT) or premature (P). Give details of any abnormalities present in the child at birth (e.g. spina bifida, mongolism, etc) and of any particular circumstances surrounding the birth (such as prolonged labour, induction, breach birth, etc).

Medical history. Enter here any details known of the medical history of the child since birth, including the occurrence of 'failure to thrive'.

Accommodation. Enter here the following details of the accommodation occupied by the family of the subject child at the time of registration:

i   *Number of rooms.* Enter here the number of rooms used by the household for eating, sleeping or living in. Do not include bathrooms, toilets, halls or small kitchens (i.e. those that cannot be used for eating in).

ii *Time in residence.* Enter here the approximate length of time the household has occupied this accommodation.

iii *Type.* Indicate the type of accommodation involved by ringing the appropriate category. In the case of a flat indicate the storey height.

iv *Tenure.* Ring the appropriate category to indicate if the household own the accommodation (or are buying it) (*O. Occ.*); if they rent it from the council, or from a New Town authority (*Council*); if they rent it unfurnished from a private landlord (including housing associations, 'tied' accommodation, rent-free accommodation) (*Rented UF*); or if they rent it furnished (*Rented F*). If none of these applies, give details.

v   *Amenities.* Indicate, by circling the key letter, if the household has exclusive use (E), shared use (S), or lacks (L) each of the following amenities:

    Cooker: excludes gas ring or appliance without oven.
    Bath: excludes those having to be filled by hand, but includes fixed shower.
    Hot water: excludes coppers where water must be transferred by hand.
    Kitchen sink: must be permanently connected; excludes wash hand basin.
    Inside WC: flush toilet with entrance inside the building.
    Outside WC: flush toilet with entrance outside the building.

vi *Date moved.* If the household changes its accommodation, this information should be entered as soon as it comes to notice. The relevant monitor should be cited if appropriate.

Finance. Enter the approximate total weekly income of the household from all sources, after tax and deductions. Note also whether the family is in receipt of Supplementary Benefits. Any changes in this position should be entered as soon as they come to notice, and the relevant monitor cited if appropriate.

Cultural factors. Note here any factors related to the ethnic background or religious orientation of the parents or caretakers of the subject child which may be relevant to their child-rearing attitudes or practices.

Stress factors. Note here any stress factors operative in the household, and in particular any factors which may have been active as a precipitating situation. These include material factors — debt, bad housing, overcrowding; personal factors — marital problems, history of psychiatric treatment; child-focused problems — slow development, handicap or behaviour problem in subject child or siblings; legal factors — pending or completed court actions; social factors — isolation from help, advice, amenities; or historical factors — events in the personal history of parents or caretakers which may be relevant.

Any other details. Note here any relevant information not elsewhere covered.

APPENDIX 4.3

Guidelines for
the management of cases
of non-accidental injury
to children in the
City of Manchester

The Manchester Child Abuse Policy Committee is set up to carry out the functions of an Area Review Committee for the City of Manchester as defined in DHSS Circular LASSL (74) 13, CMO (74) 8.

1   The Committee delegates responsibility to the NSPCC Special Unit to keep a register of all cases; to ensure that case conferences are held, where appropriate, to review periodically all notified cases. The Special Unit also provides a casework and consultation service.

2   The guidelines set out in this memorandum should be followed in all confirmed and suspected cases of non-accidental injury to children who meet the following criteria:—

All physically injured children under the age of 16 years where the nature of the injury is not consistent with the account of how it occurred or where other factors indicate that there is reasonable suspicion that the injury was inflicted or not prevented by any person having custody, charge or care of the child.

All personnel should note that it is not necessary to duplicate those procedural steps which they are certain have already been implemented by other personnel.

Cases coming to the notice of social workers

Social workers authorised under the C. & Y. P. Act, 1969

1   Immediately consult with a senior designated staff member, who will be responsible for:—

(a) Supporting and advising the social worker about the management of the case throughout these procedures and subsequently.

(b) Checking the Special Unit register, and notifying the case to the register after investigation, if appropriate.

(c) Having liaison with the Special Unit which will arrange a case conference, unless it is mutually agreed that one is unnecessary.

2   Consult with all other agencies who may have information about the child or family, including the child's general practitioner, clinical medical officer, health visitor and appropriate staff of school attended.

3   Interview the parents (or other persons having custody, charge or care of the child).

4   See the child, carefully note and record the child's condition and any observed injuries.

5   Ensure that the child receives medical diagnosis and treatment, either through the general practitioner or the casualty department.

6   Obtain a Place of Safety Order where it is necessary to afford immediate protection to the child.

7   If during step 2 it is ascertained that an authorised social worker in another agency is servicing the family, mutually agree and confirm with that worker who will carry out these procedures. If it is agreed that the other worker accepts responsibility for action as above, the social worker to whom the case was referred must satisfy himself that the other worker follows these procedures and ensure that he receives a report of any decisions made about the case. Both social workers should attend the case conference, if one is held.

Social workers who are not authorised under the C. & Y. P. Act, 1969

1   Immediately consult with a senior designated staff member who will be responsible for:—

(a) Supporting and advising the social worker about the management of the case throughout these procedures and subsequently.

(b) Checking the Special Unit register and notifying the case to the register after investigation, if appropriate.

(c) Referring the case for investigation (if necessary), either to the area office of the Social Services Department, the NSPCC inspector or the Special Unit.

2   Prepare a written report for the social worker to whom the case has been referred, and attend case conference, if held.

3   In some cases there may be considerable doubt about the diagnosis of non-accidental injury and whether the case should be referred to an authorised social worker. In these circumstances the senior designated staff member should consult with the Special Unit staff about how to proceed.

Cases coming to the notice of health visitors

1   Immediately consult with a senior designated staff member who will be responsible for:—

(a) Supporting and advising the health visitor about her future role in the case.

(b) Checking the Special Unit register and notifying the case to the register after investigation, if appropriate.

(c) Referring the case for investigation (if necessary) either to the area office of the Social Services Department, the NSPCC inspector or the Special Unit.

(d) Ensuring that the child is medically examined.

2   Consult with the child's general practitioner.

3   Consult with the child's clinical medical officer.

4   Prepare a written report for the Divisional Nursing Officer and the Nursing Officer with a copy for the Community Physician (Child Health) and the Area Nurse (Child Health).

5   In some cases there may be considerable doubt about the diagnosis of non-accidental injury and whether the case should be referred to a social worker. In these circumstances, the senior designated staff member should consult with the Special Unit staff about how to proceed.

Cases coming to the notice of school nurses

1 Immediately consult with the Nursing Officer who will be responsible for:—

    (a) Supporting and advising the school nurse about her future role in the case.

    (b) Checking the Special Unit register and notifying the case to the register after investigation, if appropriate.

    (c) Referring the case for investigation (if necessary) to the area office of the Social Services Department, the NSPCC inspector or the Special Unit.

    (d) Ensuring that the child is medically examined.

    (e) Ensuring that the heads of schools are kept informed of action taken.

2 Consult with the school medical officer.

3 Prepare a written report for the Divisional Nursing Officer and the Nursing Officer with a copy for the Community Physician (Child Health) and the Area Nurse (Child Health)

Cases coming to the notice of general practitioners, clinical medical officers, school medical officers

1 It is preferable in all cases of suspected non-accidental injury (however minor the injury), to refer the child to hospital for admission and investigation (see BMJ, 1973, 4, 656-660). The following are also available to give advice when required:—

Central & South District:
Dr. F. N. Bamford,
Senior Lecturer in Community Paediatrics,
University of Manchester,
Department of Child Health,
St. Mary's Hospital, Manchester.
(Telephone No. 061-224 9633)

North District:
Dr. J. H. Keen,
Consultant Paediatrician,
Booth Hall Children's Hospital.
(Telephone No. 061-740 2254)

If there are any difficulties in deciding what steps to take in referring the case for social management, the NSPCC Special Unit staff are available to advise.
Tel: 061-248 6060 (office hours)
     061-832 6677 (after hours emergency)

2 A check can be made of the Special Unit register to ascertain whether the child has sustained previous suspected non-accidental injury, and the case should be referred to the register, if non-accidental injury is suspected.

3 The health visitor may be able to provide additional information to assist in diagnosis, can be consulted and where applicable will have liaison with the school health service.

4 All cases can be referred to the area office of the Social Services Department, or the NSPCC inspector, or the Special Unit.

5 General practitioners and clinical medical officers are advised to keep careful records, as from time to time a medical report may be requested by the court. The appropriate fee/s will be paid by the agency requesting the report.

6 Clinical medical officers should notify the case to the Community Physician (Child Health) for central record purposes.

Cases coming to the notice of hospitals

1 Any child with a suspected non-accidental injury should be admitted to hospital. (See BMJ 1973, 4, 656-660).

2 A careful and detailed description should be written of the site and size of any bruises or other external injuries. A note should be included of the state of nutrition, cleanliness and clothing. Observation of the child's behaviour, vis-a-vis the parents and other adults should be recorded.

3 In most cases an X-ray of the skull, ribs and long bones will be desirable.

4 When bruising is a feature of the cases, appropriate tests to exclude a bleeding diatheses should be done.

5 Clinical photographs of external injuries etc. should be requested but the Medical Illustration Department should be clearly informed that they may be required for medico-legal purposes.

6 Arrange with the hospital social worker for a check to be made with the NSPCC Special Unit register, the records departments of neighbouring hospitals, the child's general practitioner and the health visitor to ascertain whether the child has suffered previous injury.

7 If the consultant in charge of the unit to which the child is admitted requires a further opinion or advice, he may ask the co-ordinating paediatrician for his assistance. The co-ordinating paediatricians are:—

Central & South District:
    Dr. F. N. Bamford,
    Senior Lecturer in Community Paediatrics,
    University of Manchester,
    Department of Child Health,
    St. Mary's Hospital,
    (Telephone No. 061-224 9633)

North District:
    Dr. J. H. Keen,
    Consultant Paediatrician,
    Booth Hall Children's Hospital,
    (Telephone No. 061-740 2254)

8 When the clinical investigations are complete a report on the findings and opinion should be prepared. In most instances a case discussion with the hospital social worker should be arranged and an appropriate course of action agreed. It is advised that careful records should be kept. They may be required in court proceedings.

9   It is preferable in all cases that the child should not be discharged without making the hospital social worker aware of this.

10   Should the parents wish to remove a child immediately and there is substantial reason to believe that the child would be in danger from this action, contact the NSPCC Special Unit—
Tel : 061-248 6060 (office hours)
061-832 6677 (after hours emergency)

Cases coming to the notice of day nursery staff

1   Suspected or confirmed cases of non-accidental injury to children are frequently referred to a day nursery by social workers, the Special Unit, health visitors, general practitioners and clinical medical officers. Children so referred are to be admitted immediately. The matron should then request a written report from the person who has referred the child. Due note should be taken of the physical condition of the child on admission. Any additional bruising, swelling or abrasions which the child sustains at a later date should be recorded in the case papers, as should the action taken by the nursery staff. Non-attendance at the nursery should be notified to the social worker supervising the family, or his or her senior.

2   When new incidents of suspected non-accidental injury (usually physical assault) come to the notice of the day nursery staff the appropriate action would be for matron (or the senior member of staff in her absence) to notify the nursery doctor, the general practitioner or the health centre to enable the child to be medically examined. The appropriate area office should also be informed. More urgent cases would justify the child's referral to the following hospitals :—

    Booth Hall
    Duchess of York
    St. Mary's   ⎱ children's department
    Wythenshawe ⎰

A letter stating all relevant details should be sent with the senior member of staff who accompanies the child to hospital, and copies sent to Dr. M. L. Bennett, Community Physician, (Child Health), Mauldeth House, the area director and the Special Unit if the child has been referred to the Unit.

3   In other cases concern may develop more gradually, and the child should be referred to the area office and the social worker concerned must be kept informed of the child's condition. If the child's condition deteriorates in any way a full written report should be submitted immediately to the area director, general practitioner and health centre.

4   When a child who is in this category is to be discharged from the day nursery to attend school, the matron should inform the head of the school concerned in writing of the relevant details, including the name of the social worker who is responsible for supervision.

Cases coming to the notice of schools

1   Non-accidental injury to children is involved in all cases of physical injury to children where the nature of the injury is not con-sistent with the account of how it occurred, or where other factors indicate that there is reasonable suspicion that the injury was inflicted or not prevented by any person having custody, charge or care of the child.

2   The appropriate action is for the head (or senior member of staff in the absence of the head) in those cases where they or any member of their staff suspects non-accidental injury to a child, to notify the school doctor or nurse.

In some cases it may be appropriate to refer children direct to one of the following children's hospitals : Booth Hall, St. Mary's, Duchess of York or Wythenshawe, and in such cases a letter must be sent to the hospital setting out the reasons for the referral. In all cases a report on the case and the action taken should be sent to the Chief Education Officer immediately. A copy of this report should be sent to the Community Physician (Child Health) at Mauldeth House, Mauldeth Road West, Manchester, M21 2RL.

3   All reports should be addressed to the Chief Education Officer, Education Offices, Crown Square, Manchester M60 3BB, marked "For the attention of Mrs. B. Fielding (Schools Branch)". The receipt of such a report will be acknowledged immediately by telephone followed by a letter, and any head not receiving an acknowledgment should telephone Mrs. Fielding at those offices, extension 7223.

4   Subsequent action is laid down in these guidelines. In brief, the action taken by the medical service will be to ensure that appropriate referrals are made to the Social Services Department or the NSPCC. You will note that the follow-up action will, where appropriate, include case conferences to which the head (or his representative), and the Chief Education Welfare Officer (or his representative) will be invited.

Cases coming to the notice of education welfare officers

1   Non-accidental injury to children is involved in all cases of physical injury to children where the nature of the injury is not con-sistent with the account of how it occurred or where other factors indicate that there is reasonable suspicion that the injury was inflicted or not prevented by any person having custody, charge or care of the child.

2   The appropriate action to be taken by any officer who suspects non-accidental injury to a child is to refer the case for investigation to the appropriate area offices of the Social Services Department or the NSPCC inspector immediately.

Following this a report on the case and the action taken must be sent to the Chief Education Officer, marked "For the attention of Mrs. B. Fielding, (Schools Branch)". This report should be submitted in the first instance to the Chief Education Welfare Officer. The receipt of such a report will be acknowledged immediately by telephone followed by a letter and any education welfare officer not receiving an acknowledgment should telephone Mrs. B. Fielding at these offices, extension 7223. A copy of this report should be sent to the appropriate area director of social services.

3   In some cases there may be considerable doubt about the diagnosis of non-accidental injury and whether the case should be referred to the area offices of the social services or the

NSPCC inspector. In these circumstances the welfare officer should bring the matter to the attention of his divisional area officer who should consult with the Special Unit staff about how to proceed.

4 Subsequent action is laid down in these guidelines. You will note that the follow-up action will, where appropriate, include case conferences to which the Chief Education Welfare Officer (or his representative) will be invited.

Police procedures

1 Area review committees have been arranged at the request of the Department of Health and Social Security. Interested organisations will be represented to determine policy and to ensure effective machinery exists to deal with the problem of non-accidental injury to children. The Chief Constable will be represented on area review committees by the Area Detective Chief Superintendent and Policewoman Chief Superintendent (or their nominees of the rank of superintendent).

2 The Policewoman Chief Superintendent will arrange for representation at any case conference to which the police are invited.

3 It will be the policy of the Chief Constable to co-operate as much as possible with the agencies involved in this matter and to this end in every case in which an assault on a child by a parent or guardian is reported, a decision to prosecute must be approved by a senior detective officer not below the rank of superintendent, or in the case of 'L', 'M' and 'N' Divisions the Detective Chief Inspector in command of Criminal Investigation Department.

4 Senior Criminal Investigation Department officers should ensure there is consultation with the appropriate agencies in these matters and in cases where a prosecution seems unnecessary, e.g. minor assaults not causing serious injury, assaults by pregnant mothers etc. — help or supervision for the parent, guardian and family will undoubtedly be arranged.

5 It is, however, to be borne in mind that the Chief Constable's right to decide on prosecutions must not be eroded in any way or by any undertakings given on his behalf.

6 Cases of special difficulty should be referred to the Chief Superintendent, Criminal Investigation Department who may consult the Assistant Chief Constable (Crime) if the necessity arises.

Case conferences

1 As soon as possible, following referral, the Special Unit should be consulted and they will ensure that a case conference is convened, where appropriate.

2 The case conference should bring together all those who can provide information about the child and his family, who have responsibility

for the safety of the child and for providing services.

3 The primary functions of the case conference are to make a diagnosis, formulate a plan of action, and decide who shall accept primary responsibility for the social management of the case. It is recognised that each agency must retain the right to act independently in accordance with their own agency policy, but every effort should be made to reach mutually agreed policies, and avoid unilateral action.

4 A case conference should always be held before any child is returned home from statutory care. If the child is in hospital or in voluntary care, the case conference should be held before discharge if time allows, but if not then as soon as possible after discharge.

Review of cases

All cases notified to the register will be reviewed by the Special Unit staff at three monthly intervals, and further action initiated whenever requested or indicated.

Special Unit register

A case register is maintained by the Special Unit and 24 hour access is available to all doctors and senior designated staff members, as listed. A 'ring-back' procedure is followed so that authenticity of callers can be checked.

N.S.P.C.C. Special Unit,
5 Wynnstay Grove,
Fallowfield, Manchester M14 6XG.
Tel : 061-248 6060 (office hours)
        061-832 6677 (after hours emergency)

Senior designated staff

SOCIAL SERVICES DEPARTMENT
Senior social workers
Principal social workers
Diagnostic social workers
Area directors at the social services area offices :

Area 1	Tel :	061-228 3851
Area 2	,,	061-223 9641
Area 3	,,	061-224 0612
Area 4	,,	061-881 0911
Area 5	,,	061-434 4611
Area 6	,,	061-499 2121

Hospital : Senior and principal social workers

NSPCC
North Group:
    Group Officer F. Thompson,
    Tel : 061-643 0916
South Group:
    Group Officer L. Morris,
    Tel : 061-224 3366

PROBATION DEPARTMENT
The Chief Probation Officer
Deputy Chief Probation Officer
Assistant chief probation officers
Senior probation officers

FAMILY WELFARE ASSOCIATION
Miss M. Harrison
Mr. T. Tomlinson
Mr. J. L. Hesketh

FAMILY SERVICE UNIT
Miss B. Callin
Mr. E. H. Thomas

CATHOLIC RESCUE SOCIETY
Miss I. Windmuller

HEALTH VISITORS
Divisional nursing officers
Nursing officers
Area Nursing Officer (Child Health)

A number of signs may pinpoint child abuse

Most injuries to children are accidental and can be simply explained.

The knocks, the cuts, the bruises and the scrapes or even the broken arm and leg, are all part of the rough and tumble of a child's life. Accidents can happen at home, in the street, or in the playground.

But a few children who have got bumps and bruises didn't simply fall downstairs or off the kitchen chair. Their injuries have been inflicted by adults, usually their parents.

Child abuse is not new. But it has received increased attention in the newspapers and on the television. Today, we are a lot more concerned and aware of the problem. Hopefully, we are more able to help the child and his or her parents.

Children can be badly- sometimes fatally- hurt by adults (perhaps at the end of their tether) shaking, hitting, dropping, squeezing, or crushing them. Or by twisting or pulling their limbs. Children can be burned by cigarettes. A child can be belted or beaten or sat in freezing or scalding water.

The problem is identifying the "abused" or "battered" child as distinct from other children.

Research into child abuse tells us that minor injuries deliberately inflicted may well be the beginning of increasingly more serious injuries. A child abused once is likely to be abused again. Brothers and sisters may be at risk too.

There are a number of signs which, in combination, may help to pinpoint the abused child. They are:

● the appearance of unexplained fractures, cuts or bruises. It is easy for the child who is crawling or walking to get cuts or bruises; it is not so easy for babies. An unlikely explanation could be an indicator of child abuse.

● the repeated incidence of minor injuries. This is especially important if the reasons are unexplained or unlikely.

● Fractures, burns, scalds, lacerations and swellings without adequate explanation.

● Frequently child abuse is accompanied by the child's failure to thrive. Loss of weight or slowness in reaching the developmental milestones may be indicators.

● Unexplained absences, at regular intervals, from nursery or school.

● Lethargy, tiredness or withdrawal or very aggressive tendencies may point to a history of ill-treatment.

● the attitude of parents is important. The parent may hand the child in an unfeeling or mechanical way.

Many parents, who may abuse their children, are suspicious of
authority and don't visit schools or attend clinics. Some, on
the other hand, are quite the opposite. They may frequently
approach a variety of people with seemingly trivial
difficulties. with their child. Accompanied by unexplained
injuries, this could be a cry for help and advice.

Usually, parents, who have been known to abuse their
children, are a little immature and don't happily enjoy their
role as a mum or a dad. It is likely that they, themselves, may
have been the subject of abuse in childhood.

It is important to note that the "battered" or "abused" child
can be of any age or any social group. The younger the child,
often the more serious the injuries. And the researchers say that
more boys rather than girls are abused.

To think of every child with a cut, or a bruise, or a black eye
as being an abused child would be wrong. But those working
with children may be worried, from time to time, about those
injuries or absences which are unexplained or where the
explanation is unlikely.

After careful thought, if you are concerned about a child,
ask for expert advice. Manchester is fortunate to have
specialist services to help both children and parents.

Social workers from the City's Social Services Department or
from the National Society for the Prevention of Cruelty to
Children cannot, it must be emphasised, remove a child from
the care of his or her parents without an
Order from the Court. In approximately
one in five cases, such a step may be
necessary, but cannot be undertaken
without adequate evidence.

There is a set of guidelines on the
procedures of what to do to enlist
the appropriate services. These
guidelines are readily available. A copy
can be obtained from the City's Social
Services Department, Solway House,
Aytoun Street, Manchester.
M1 3ET.

APPENDIX 4.5
REGISTER OF SUSPECTED NON-ACCIDENTAL INJURY TO CHILDREN

NSPCC SPECIAL UNIT (   )

STRICTLY CONFIDENTIAL

INDEX NO:
MONITOR NO:

Date sent out: Date returned:

Child's Name: .... d.o.b. .... M/F.

Address: ....

G.P. .... Tel: .... School: .... Tel: ....

The above child was notified to the register on.................................... and the following details of
suspected non-accidental injury/at risk circumstances were noted:

....

....

This case was last reviewed on..
Could you please now review your record of this child, since this date, and provide the following
information:—

1.   Has any further information emerged which confirms or excludes a diagnosis of non-accidental
       injury or at risk circumstances in this case?   YES/NO
1a.   If yes, give details: ....

....

---

2.   Has a case conference been held during the period under review? YES/NO
2a   If yes, Date: .... Venue: ....

2b   What recommendations were made? ....

....

....

2c.   Have these recommendations been implemented? ....

....

....

---

3.   Has any court action been taken in this case?

       Adult Court: YES/NO.   If yes, by whom: Local Authority/NSPCC/Police
       Result: ....

★
3a.   Are any other legal proceedings pending or completed which affect this family? YES/NO.
       if yes, give details: ....

....

3b.   Are there any court orders in force in respect of this child? (Specify)

....

....

....

★ Juvenile Court: YES/NO.   If yes, by whom: Local Authority/NSPCC/Police
Result: ....

4. Has this child received any subsequent injuries which you think may be non-accidental; NO/YES.
4a. If yes, give details:

....

....

....

5. Do you consider this child to be still at risk?   NO/YES.
5a. If yes, give details:

....

....

6. Is the child: at home/in care/in hospital/other (specify)
6a. If at home, is the child attending: Nursery school/day nursery/playgroup/day school/other (specify)

   If yes, give address:

7. Who is visiting this family? Give agency and name of each worker:

....

....

8. Have any of the following circumstances altered over this period? If yes, give full details:
8a. Address.   NO/YES

....

8b. Child's parents or caretakers.   NO/YES

....

8c. Those living in the household.   NO/YES

....

8d. Occupational circumstances.   NO/YES

....

8e. Financial circumstances.   NO/YES

....

8f. Other changes or relevant information:

....

9. Have any other children in this family received injuries over this period which you think may be non-accidental?   NO/YES
9a. If yes, give details:

....

....

10. Do you consider any other member of the family to be at risk?   NO/YES
10a. If yes, give details:

....

....

Completed by: Address: Tel:

Bert L. Raisbeck   *Lawyer*

5   THE LEGAL FRAMEWORK

In this chapter an examination will be undertaken of the protection available and remedies open to children and spouses who are being subjected to physical violence. Merely as a means of approaching the legal framework it will be convenient to examine two types of situation, respectively that of the battered child and that of the battered spouse. Often these are part of the one syndrome, and too often the fearful and oppressed wife will consequently decline to make any approach to the authorities about her violent husband. Again, reference will be made throughout to the battered wife or violent husband but merely for the sake of simplicity — our society is not without husbands who need protection from their wives.

VIOLENCE TO CHILDREN

Under the law there is ample protection for children who are physically ill treated or neglected, who are exposed to moral danger, or whose proper development is being avoidably prevented or neglected. Given any hypothetical situation in which a child is being ill treated, there will invariably be a legal solution; obviously he requires more protection under the law than an adult person, and in the case of the child there must be more provision for some interested party to intervene on his behalf and set the legal machinery in motion. This social intervention can take the form of a criminal prosecution of the person responsible; civil proceedings resulting in formal supervision of the situation or removal of the child from his environment; a judicial decision by the local authority without there necessarily being court proceedings; and finally the law caters for the emergency or crisis situation where the unavoidable delay in obtaining a court order could be fatal.

Criminal proceedings
Although the law still permits parents to chastise their children in moderation, once there is a degree of immoderacy there is the possibility of criminal proceedings. Apart from the general criminal law contained in the Offences against the Person Act, 1861, under which any person may be

prosecuted for a criminal assault, there are special provisions regarding children contained in Part I of the Children and Young Persons Act, 1933 (as amended by the Children and Young Persons Act, 1963). Section I of the 1933 Act gives some indication of the width of the provisions:

> If any person who has attained the age of sixteen years and has the custody, charge or care of any child or young person under that age wilfully assaults, ill treats, neglects, abandons or exposes him, or causes or procures him to be assaulted, ill treated neglected, abandoned, or exposed, in a manner likely to cause him unnecessary suffering or injury to health . . . that person shall be guilty . . .

This provision protects juveniles under the age of sixteen years, but renders liable to prosecution not only the parents but any person of sixteen years or over who has the 'custody, charge or care'; for example, it would include the baby-sitter to whom the parent had delegated his powers and duties. The parent who so delegated to a person known to him to be a child-beater would himself be liable under this Act for 'causing or procuring'. In addition, it is not vital for a prosecution that there be a physical attack on the child or young person; 'ill treats . . . in a manner likely to cause him unnecessary suffering or injury to health' could include continual threats of violence, and in addition would catch in its net the sadistic wife-beater who makes his children watch his attacks. In these situations, where there is no physical attack on the child, his particular characteristics (e.g. fortitude, nervous disposition, etc) will be taken into account to determine whether there is potential suffering or injury to health — 'health' including mental health in this context.

In a recent prosecution under this section an infant had suffered injuries which the court was satisfied were likely to have been sustained by blows. Both parents denied responsibility; they were charged jointly and both were convicted of wilfully ill treating the child. The appeal court upheld their conviction; they were *jointly in charge* of the child at the material times. (Marsh *v.* Hodgson, (1974) *Criminal Law Review* 35.)

Prosecutions under this Act are generally brought by the NSPCC or the police. The reluctance of local authorities to prosecute is understandable if one is thinking merely in terms of fines or imprisonment (a maximum of six months in the magistrates' court, two years in the Crown court). However, although prison might be considered appropriate in cases of cold-blooded, calculated cruelty, the courts should be prepared to consider the family as a whole and think in terms of expert supervision. Since the social worker cannot accurately foretell the outcome of prosecutions he may well be loath to institute them and prefer to consider civil proceedings in the juvenile court — 'care' proceedings.

Care proceedings
The Children and Young Persons Act, 1969, stipulates the conditions
which must prevail before the court can make an order in respect of a
child or young person in respect of whom care proceedings are brought
in the juvenile court. Apart from the need for care or control six
'primary conditions' are outlined in section 1, and the court must be
satisfied that at least one of them prevails. Two are concerned with
violence in the family.

Section 1(2)(a) provides for the situation where the child's 'proper
development is being avoidably prevented or neglected or his health is
being avoidably impaired or neglected or he is being ill treated'. Obviously
this includes physical attacks, but it will also apply to any course of
conduct likely to cause injury, whether physical or mental.

Given, then, that there appears to be sufficient evidence to satisfy the
juvenile court as to ill treatment, and a need for care or control which is
unlikely to be met unless an order is made, the court may make an order
giving the local authority Social Services Department or a probation
officer the right to supervise the child in the family, such supervision order
being capable of continuing until the age of eighteen. Alternatively – and
more likely if there is a history of ill treatment and a probability of its
continuance – the court can make an order committing the child or young
person to the care of the local authority. Again, the order can continue
until the age of eighteen, but in this case the Social Services Department
assumes much more control; in effect the local authority is given almost all
the rights of a parent, and – most important – can, without any further
trips to the juvenile court, either accommodate the juvenile in a community
home or foster home or, as circumstances alter substantially, send him back
to his parents. The latter step is not taken lightly in the case of physical
violence. Even if the local authority permits the child to reside at home he
continues to be in their care until such time as the juvenile court revokes
or varies the care order (which may be on the application of the local
authority or the parent or guardian).

Section 1(2)(a) deals with an existing situation – the child '*is being* ill
treated'. If the Act made no further provision the social worker would be in
the invidious position of having to make application in care proceedings *after*
each of several children in the family had been ill treated, and this could
have dire consequences for those remaining after the first care order had
been made. Section 1(2)(b) envisages this sort of situation, and states:

It is probable that the conditions set out in [section 1(2)(a)] will be satisfied in his
case, having regard to the fact that the court or another court has found that

condition is or was satisfied in the case of another child or young person who is or was a member of the household to which he belongs.

In other words, where one child in the family is ill treated, and there is a *likelihood* that others of that household *will* be ill treated, the court can make a care order in respect of them all, regardless of the fact that there has not yet been an attack on the rest. This is an eminently sensible provision – a prophylactic measure rather than an attempted cure which might be too late. There is, apparently, a gap in the law despite this useful provision: although it covers the typical situation where one child is attacked and it is considered necessary to remove the rest from the household, it does not cover one sort of situation which is not uncommon. Where an inveterate child-beater well known to the social services *leaves* his wife and children and forms an illicit union with a woman who already has children of ages approximating those of the children beaten in the other household, section 1(2)(b) would appear not to apply because of its restriction to the same household. Given this situation, those interested in the welfare of children who are at risk must wait until there is ill treatment before they can intervene. There may be a conflict between children's welfare and parental rights; if so it must be resolved in favour of the child at risk. A widening of the scope of section 1(2)(b) would not come amiss – the decision whether or not to make an order is the court's, but at least the interested authority should be able to bring to the attention of the court situations where there is serious *risk* of injury.

Emergency situations

Although there is not usually much delay between the initiation of action and the hearing in the juvenile court, in certain conditions speed is of the essence if the life or well-being of the child is not to be jeopardised. Such situations of urgency are catered for by the law, which provides for the lawful detention of children and young persons for a period up to a maximum of twenty-eight days without the need for a court appearance and any consequent delay this might entail.

Place of safety order. Section 28 of the Children and Young Persons Act, 1969, stipulates that 'any person' can apply to a magistrate for a place-of-safety order. If the magistrate is satisfied that the applicant has reasonable cause to believe that certain conditions set out in section 1 of the Act are satisfied in respect of the child or young person, then he may grant the place of safety order. The 'primary conditions' in section 1 obviously include neglect and ill treatment; also covered is the prophylactic measure in section 1(2)(b) referred to above.

The application to the magistrate need not be in court, and in practice rarely will be. The person involved in the application will invariably be a local authority social worker – and the order will normally be needed at about 2.00 a.m.! It is a matter of having a working relationship (and the home address and telephone number) with at least one of the local Justices of the Peace. There is no need to observe any legal formality; all that is required is that the applicant inform the Justice orally of the facts, sufficient to satisfy him that there is reasonable cause to believe neglect, ill treatment, etc. At this stage there is no need to consider the need for care or control, merely the primary condition.

If the Justice grants the application, then the child or young person in respect of whom the application has been made can be lawfully detained in a place of safety for a maximum of twenty-eight days (or any shorter period specified in the place of safety order). At the end of the specified period the child must be released unless an order of the court has been obtained.

The order will be applied for in a time of crisis – the infant child found apparently abandoned, showing signs of ill treatment or neglect, there being no indication of the presence of parents or any other adults in charge. Section 28 is itself a prophylactic measure in that this initial step of lawful detention of the child or young person in a place of safety (usually a community home) is taken as a result of a quick evaluation of a given situation. As soon as practicable the parent or guardian should be informed of the whereabouts of his child and the reason for the detention; there is no requirement for an application to the juvenile court in care proceedings as an automatic second step. The place of safety order authorises the removal and detention of the child, and gives the appropriate authorities time to make a total evaluation. If it is considered that the crisis has passed, or that it is in the interests of the child that he be returned home, then at any time during the currency of the order the child may be released from the place of safety.

Although, in time, a more thorough assessment of the total situation may reveal that there is no cause for alarm, this does not affect the legality of the detention under the order and is in itself no reflection on the social worker's decision to apply for the order in the first instance. Occasionally one senses anxiety among social workers regarding section 28 applications, exacerbated by the ill founded belief that detention in a place of safety automatically means that there must be an application later to the juvenile court; this results in a disinclination to approach a Justice in a given situation despite the social worker's fears for the child's welfare. Undue deliberation about the care or control test, false imprisonment of the child or the ability to satisfy one's seniors the next day that one's assessment was correct does not work in the child's best interests. A place of safety order in itself constitutes the detention lawful, and itself gives authority to refute any claims the parent may take for the return of the child; and all that is necessary in order to obtain this power under the law is 'reasonable cause to believe' that the child is being ill treated, etc. Better to act in what appears to be the child's best interests by a lawful removal to a place of safety, and accept that in the cold light of dawn, when more facts will be known, that the correct decision might then be to return the child to his parents — better that than inactivity through over-caution, anxiety or ignorance of the law, and the discovery the following day that it is now too late to take action to prevent serious injury or worse.

Place of safety warrant. Where it is considered that a child or young person is the victim of any assault, ill treatment or neglect such as is likely to cause unnecessary suffering or injury to health, or is the victim of any of the crimes listed in the First Schedule to the Children and Young Persons Act, 1933, then a constable may be authorised to remove the child or young person to a place of safety by a warrant issued by a Justice under section 40 of the 1933 Act.

The place of safety warrant can be issued by the Justice (again, there is no requirement for this to be in court) on an application by any person acting in the child's interests — but it authorises a police constable to remove the child. The social worker may well be the first to be involved in a situation which gives grounds for belief that a child is being ill treated; if it is a matter of forcible removal of the child, or forcible entry into the home to seize him from the offending parent — in fact any situation where it appears that force will be necessary and there will be some breach of the peace, or any entry into premises against the will of the occupier, then the social worker should collaborate with the police and take joint action. The constable must be named in the place of safety warrant. Therefore in this given situation the social worker and constable will often visit the Justice together; the social worker will state the facts and the Justice, if satisfied, will issue the warrant authorising the constable to enter and seize the child and remove him to a place of safety, or alternatively to enter and satisfy himself that the condition exists and *then* remove the child to the place of safety. A warrant of the latter type will be issued when there is evidence giving cause for concern, but it is not as strong as in the more clear-cut situation of violence.

Again, the child may be detained for a period up to twenty-eight days, by which time either he must be released or an order of the court must have been obtained to make any further detention against the wishes of the parent lawful. The social worker who gives the information to the Justice is entitled to accompany the constable who goes to execute the warrant (unless, exceptionally, the warrant excludes him expressly). In addition the warrant may stipulate that a medical practitioner accompany the constable; in all cases of removal of children to a place of safety because ill treatment is suspected it is advisable that a doctor be present at the time of the removal, as his evidence could be crucial in later proceedings in court. If it is not practicable to have a doctor present, the child should be medically examined as soon as possible — primarily to ensure that he receives any attention necessary, and secondarily to obtain evidence for court (not to mention refuting any claim by the parent that the injuries were suffered in the place of safety, not at home!).

Again, all that the law requires of the applicant is reasonable cause to suspect, and in two particular instances the law states that a refusal to allow a child to be visited or premises to be inspected constitutes such reasonable cause for the purposes of a section 40 warrant. The two instances are those of the foster child (section 8, Children Act, 1958) and the child placed for adoption who has become a 'protected child' (section 45, Adoption Act, 1958). A refusal to permit an authorised officer to visit the child, or to inspect the premises, in addition to being a criminal offence automatically gives sufficient cause for concern for a Justice to authorise a constable to enter (by force where necessary) and search for the child and if necessary remove him from the home to a place of safety. These two particular instances reinforce the general implication, so far as the law is concerned, that a reasonable belief that a child is being ill treated is sufficient justification for his detention and removal to a place of safety, or his seizure and removal to a place of safety. Social workers have no power to use force to enter premises (the law being loath to give private citizens or officials any powers to invade the property or person of others except where it is considered vital). The police have such powers in appropriate circumstances, and can be called upon to assist where it is anticipated that violent resistance will be encountered.

Section 28 of the 1969 Act gives the police wider powers than those allowed to social workers, in that a constable may detain a child or young person on his own initiative (without authorisation by a Justice of the Peace) if he has reasonable cause to believe that any of four primary conditions of section 1 of the Act apply, including, obviously, the ill treatment condition. Where there is such detention, there must be an enquiry by a police officer not below the rank of inspector, or an officer

in charge of a police station, and that officer must either release the child
or young person or else make arrangements for his detention in a place
of safety for a period not exceeding eight days. A certificate signed by
the police officer is sufficient authorisation in these circumstances for the
local authority to refute the claims of the parents if the child or young
person is detained in a community home.

Assumption of parental rights

Section 1 of the Children Act, 1948, lists the circumstances where the
local authority is under a duty to receive a juvenile under the age of
seventeen into care, these circumstances including the situation where
the juvenile has no parent or guardian, or where the parent or guardian is
prevented from providing for his proper accommodation, maintenance
and upbringing (either temporarily or permanently; the reason being mental
or physical or other incapacity).

Provided a child is already voluntarily in care under section 1 (there
being no power to take the child against the wishes of the parent) the local
authority may by resolution assume parental rights over him provided
any of certain conditions are satisfied. These conditions include the parent's
being of such habits or mode of life as to make him unfit to have the care
of the child. In addition, if the parent suffers from a mental disorder
rendering him unfit to have care, then parental rights may be assumed
by the authority. A resolution under section 2 of the 1948 Act might
therefore be passed in a situation where, although there has been no ill
treatment of the child, it is feared that there is a substantial risk if he is
returned to the parent. Provided the child is already voluntarily in the
care of the authority, and provided the authority can, in the event, satisfy
the juvenile court that one of the conditions in section 2 is satisfied, then
preventive action can be taken by this assumption of parental rights in
appropriate circumstances. Even though no section 2 resolution is in
force, the child being voluntarily in the care of the authority, the authority
is not obliged to surrender him to the parent on the latter's request if it is
considered that to do so would be contrary to the child's interests.

The procedure laid down in the 1948 Act must be rigidly adhered to if
the resolution of the authority is to be effective. Notice of the resolution
and its effect must be served on the parent, who must also be informed
of his right to object in writing within one month. If a written objection
is received, then within fourteen days of receipt the authority must
complain to the juvenile court and justify its decision, otherwise the
resolution lapses. If there is no objection from the parent within the month
the resolution continues in force until the child reaches the age of eighteen

or until either the authority rescinds it or the parent applies successfully to the juvenile court for rescission.

The effect of the resolution is largely the same as that of a care order made by the juvenile court. The authority can decide where the juvenile is to live, and in both cases he may be returned to his parents without the authority losing the right to demand his return. Such a step would not be taken lightly, especially when there has been any question of physical ill treatment. A wide discretion is now vested in local authorities in respect of children committed to care by the courts or in care by virtue of the authority's resolution, and normally the courts will not interfere with the decision taken by the authority as to where the child should live (i.e. in a community home, with foster parents, relatives or parents). Only where there is some dispute between foster parents and local authority regarding physical custody of the child do the courts tend to be involved, and then they will not usually interfere with the exercise of discretion by the authority unless there is some abuse.

An awesome responsibility consequently devolves on local authorities. The philosophy of a deal of relevant child legislation is that the best environment for the child is its natural home, and the aim of the Social Services Departments of the authorities should be to return the child initially on a trial basis rather than run the risk of institutionalising him. The initial decision having often been taken by the court, all future decisions are taken by the social workers — especially the nail-biting one whether to return home on a trial basis a child who has been the victim of ill treatment. If this discretion were to be removed from the local authority, if an order of the court were needed before a child in care could be sent home on trial, the decision would still have to be made, and the court would act largely on reports presented by the social worker involved with the family. Such a change in the law would prevent hasty decisions — but one trusts that no such decision is taken without due deliberation.

There is ample legislation to protect those who cannot protect themselves. Powers and duties are bestowed by the law on local authorities, police and other authorised bodies such as the NSPCC. Almost every conceivable situation is catered for by the various statutes — physical and mental suffering; lack of proper development; moral danger; lack of proper care or control; non-attendance at school; numerous situations specifically mentioned in the First Schedule to the 1933 Act. Yet the vulnerable are not always removed from harm; deaths make headlines, especially where the child in care has been returned home by the authority; physical injuries and psychological scars often go undetected in that no action is taken to bring the issue before the courts. How often, one wonders, is it because there has not been collaboration and co-operation between interested parties?

DISSEMINATION OF INFORMATION

Occasionally cases come to light where many individuals each have part of the evidence of physical violence. The social worker, the doctor, the teacher, the education welfare officer, the health visitor and many others each hold a piece of the jigsaw in their hand but the pieces have never been put together to obtain the full picture. Too often the watchword is 'confidentiality', and there is too acute an awareness of the confidential nature of information received. Alternatively one party mistrusts another. For example, the social worker might have his suspicions of parental activities but divulge nothing to the police because he fears the result will be a prosecution of the parents whereas he wants to create a proper atmosphere in which a working relationship with the family can be built up in the interests of the children.

The law, perhaps in a negative way, encourages the interchange of information in this context. It recognises the conflict between confidentiality on the one hand and the interests of the child on the other. So far as court proceedings are concerned, the only confidential relationship recognised by the law is that between solicitor and client. This relationship is privileged in the sense that, in general, the solicitor is not obliged to divulge the content of communications between himself and his client unless the client waives the privilege. The relationship of doctor and patient, priest and penitent, social worker and client, etc, is not similarly privileged — so information obtained in confidence would have to be divulged where the court required the truth. Outside the courtroom the interchange of relevant information is encouraged in that, provided the person giving the information is under a duty (not necessarily a legal duty) to give it, and the person to whom it is given has a recognised legal interest in receiving it, there need be no fear of any libel suit in the civil courts if by chance an allegation contained in a report should happen to be unfounded. Provided there is no malice, one need not feel inhibited, so far as the law is concerned, in reporting one's suspicions and fears to any party who has a legal interest in receiving such information.

In general the law does not impose a duty on any class of individuals to make reports to anyone of their suspicions; it is difficult to see how such legislation could be enforced were it to be passed. The law cannot in reality demand that information be disseminated, since this must in the

on the assessment made by and the decision taken by
...cerned with the child whose general demeanour or
...condition gives cause for concern. There is a moral
...formation where the welfare of a child is at stake, and
...his duty to impart information to interested parties
...by protecting from civil suit those who in good faith cast aspersions on
the character of the parent by alleging that he or she might be responsible
for injuries to the child, even though the allegation proves to be unfounded.

VIOLENCE TO SPOUSES

Whereas the law makes provision for interested persons to intercede on
behalf of children subjected to violence, since they will often not be in a
position to obtain the protection of the law, in the case of the wife
subjected to violence at the hands of her husband the attitude of the law
is generally the same as in any situation where an adult person is attacked.
Remedies are available to the wife, but usually she will be expected to
initiate action herself. Whether she will be capable of such action or in a
position where she dares take it is another question.

In theory, then, the battered wife can always invoke the legal machinery
and obtain protection against the violent husband. If a serious crime of
violence is committed against her, or if there has been a serious breach
of the peace, then a criminal prosecution may be brought without the
wife taking the initiative.

Any attack by the husband causing the wife any actual bodily harm
constitutes a criminal offence. The harm need not be serious — in fact if
the wife is wounded (the slightest breaking of the skin being sufficient) or
suffers really serious bodily harm, then the husband can be convicted of a
much more serious offence. If criminal proceedings are brought, the wife
is a competent and compellable witness against her own husband — but if
she is an unwilling witness (which might well be the case if there has been
a reconciliation since the attack), then the police may well be hard put to
prove the charge. Understandably, as a result of bitter experience, the
police are perhaps loath to interfere in domestic disputes unless there is
a grave risk of bodily injury or serious crime has been committed.

If the police are unwilling to initiate proceedings the wife may herself
complain to the magistrates. This might have a deterrent effect on her
husband, or it might be counter-productive!

Again, just like any other adult person who is not in any special
relationship with her attacker, the wife may bring a civil action in the

tort of battery. For this purpose the Law Reform (Husband and Wife) Act, 1962, removed some of the vestiges of Victorian thinking from matrimonial law and permitted the wife to bring such an action against her husband, the legislators accepting that the husband and wife should be treated as separate legal persons with the right to sue each other. The award of damages for any injury suffered will not usually be an end in itself. Having started such a civil action, the wife could apply for an injunction — and this latter might well be the primary object in bringing the tort action, since it will give her a measure of legal protection and should have some deterrent effect on the husband, who will have been made aware of the serious consequences of breach of the injunction. The availability of injunctions and their efficacy will be examined within the context of matrimonial law, since this governs the majority of the situations where there is violence towards the spouse.

Matrimonial proceedings

The magistrates' court. The wife who wants some speedy (and perhaps interim) relief will complain to the magistrates' court, which will sit as a domestic court to hear the complaint. *Persistent* cruelty is a matrimonial offence for this purpose and would entitle the wife to relief. However, 'persistent' denotes some degree of continuity: one isolated attack would not constitute persistent cruelty. If a single attack has resulted in the husband's being convicted in the Crown court, or in his being sentenced to at least one month's imprisonment by the magistrates, then this would constitute a matrimonial offence entitling the wife to relief.

Given that the husband has committed such a matrimonial offence, the wife would be justified in leaving the matrimonial home and would not be in desertion. This, however, presupposes that she has alternative accommodation, and this aspect will be examined later. The magistrates may grant a separation order to the wife, and will be prepared to do so particularly in a situation where the matrimonial offence she proves is one of persistent cruelty. However, the effect of the order is merely to relieve the spouses of the marital duty to cohabit. The wife, having been granted a separation order, can refuse to cohabit with her husband, and will not thereby be in desertion, as she is merely exercising a right which the order gives her. Similarly she can legally refuse to have sexual intercourse with her husband — if he insists on exercising this 'marital right' without her consent he will be guilty not only of any assault which takes place but also of rape. The separation order, or non-cohabitation clause, does not, therefore, afford much protection to the battered wife.

The magistrates should have the power in such cases to make a non-molestation order, i.e. an injunction forbidding the husband from molesting his wife in any way on pain of imprisonment for wilful disobedience.

If the wife has somewhere for herself, and any children, to reside, and she leaves the matrimonial home, her application to the magistrates will usually be for a maintenance order and custody order in addition to any separation order. She must satisfy the magistrates that her husband's conduct was expulsive, otherwise she will be in desertion and consequently not entitled to maintenance. In the case of the battered wife there should be little difficulty in satisfying the court on this score. However, as the law stands the magistrates have no jurisdiction, however serious the situation, to make a non-molestation order — and in many cases it is this sort of legal protection that the wife wants.

The divorce court. Although the magistrates' court can make a separation order, or award the wife custody of children and maintenance for herself and the children, it has no jurisdiction to dissolve a marriage. An undefended divorce petition is within the jurisdiction of the county court; if the petition is defended the case will be transferred to the High Court. The wife of a violent man would have to satisfy the divorce court that her husband 'has behaved in such a way that [she] cannot reasonably be expected to live with [him]', in addition to which the court would have to be satisfied that the marriage had broken down irretrievably. (During the first three years of marriage the parties can be divorced only if it is shown that the case is one of exceptional hardship suffered by the petitioner or of exceptional depravity on the part of the respondent. If this cannot be proved the parties are bound to each other in law until three years have elapsed.) The wife, having obtained her divorce, will then have the same redress at law as any citizen would have against another in the event of her ex-husband assaulting her.

But the wife who is being subjected to violence may not wish to petition for divorce. She may consider that with help and guidance the marriage can be saved and is worth saving. In any event, she is likely to be emotionally disturbed and in no position to make a rational decision as to whether or not to terminate her marriage. Her immediate need is for protection and accommodation, both for herself and for any children of the marriage; usually the wife will not wish to share the matrimonial home with her violent husband. Either his vacating the home, or the availability to her of alternative accommodation, is the immediate solution. Whether or not this can be achieved, the wife will want an injunction from the court ordering the husband not to molest her.

The non-molestation injunction

Section 45 of the Supreme Court of Judicature (Consolidation) Act, 1925, states that the High Court has power to grant an injunction in all cases in which it appears to the court to be just or convenient so to do. This provision would appear to give the High Court an uninhibited power to grant to the battered wife a non-molestation order; however, the courts have interpreted the provision narrowly, just as they have similarly restricted the scope of section 74 of the County Courts Act, 1959, which gives a like power to the county courts. The restriction imposed by judicial interpretation means that the battered wife cannot obtain a non-molestation order unless her application arises in the course of pending proceedings in the respective courts. In other words, the judges have decided that the two statutes did not give them the power one might assume. The wife who requires a non-molestation order must have begun proceedings in the High Court or the county court to terminate her marriage, or must have begun High Court proceedings for a decree of judicial separation; only if such a petition has been filed or, exceptionally, if the wife undertakes to file such a petition will the court grant an injunction.

The sanction for breach of an injunction is committal to prison. The granting of an injunction ordering the husband not to molest his wife could therefore have a salutary effect on him and would invariably act as a serious deterrent should he consider further violence towards his wife. The judges, however, do not seem to be aware as yet of the need which the battered wife has of protection under the law, nor of the fact that the insistence on the commencement of proceedings to terminate the marriage obviously militates against reconciliation, whereas the aim of modern family legislation is reconciliation rather than dissolution, where this can be achieved. If divorce proceedings are begun, the chance of reconciliation is obviously more remote than if the wife were allowed to apply for a non-molestation order to restrain her husband from further attacks, the courts being prepared to grant such an application without insistence on its being ancillary to other matrimonial proceedings.

However, this notion of the injunction application's being ancillary to some substantive action is now embedded in the law and has been accepted by the Court of Appeal; the wide discretion can be returned to the courts only by statute or by a decision of the Appellate Committee of the House of Lords overruling the existing restrictive judicial interpretations. If the magistrates' courts are to have the power to make non-molestation orders, the change will require an Act of Parliament. One hopes that if such legislation is to be passed the legislators will take the opportunity to include in the statute a reform of the law on the granting of injunctions against violent husbands.

As mentioned earlier, one course open to the wife who does not wish to take matrimonial proceedings as such is to sue her husband in the civil court (the county court or the High Court) in the tort of battery, and, immediately she has commenced the action, to apply for an injunction restraining him from future attacks. This is a method of deterring the violent spouse; better that the wife be allowed merely to apply for a non-molestation order without bringing the tort action.

Living apart

The primary need of the battered wife is invariably accommodation separate from her husband, either on a temporary basis while guidance and help are obtained, or permanently if there is no prospect of any reconciliation. In most cases the beaten wife would be afraid to remain in the same house as her husband, especially if she is setting in motion the machinery of the law, and of necessity before she can obtain any order of the court her husband must be informed. If she is present when he is informed of her complaint to the magistrates, or her petition, etc, there is every likelihood of further beating. Occasionally the knowledge that there is to be legal action will have a sobering rather than inflammatory effect — but most battered wives will not wish to take this chance and will feel compelled to make a physical break before they contemplate legal action.

If friends or relatives are willing to accommodate the wife (and the children) temporarily, she can then contemplate legal action. One of the many reforms of this decade in the sphere of matrimonial law was the abolition of the concepts of 'enticing away' or 'harbouring' wives. The helping hand can be extended without there being any risk of the husband's suing for damages. There should therefore be less inhibition about assisting the battered wife: whatever action the husband may take, he has no *legal* redress.

If the wife is not so fortunate as to have accommodating friends or relatives she will be loath to leave unless she can find somewhere to live, perhaps with the aid of a voluntary organisation or a charity. Especially if there are children of the marriage, she will be afraid of their being committed to the care of the local authority if she cannot find suitable accommodation for them. If the wife has left the matrimonial home she will not be considered homeless by the local authority unless she has taken matrimonial proceedings — this will show that her vacating the home was justified and she is therefore not in desertion. Again, then, the wife is forced to take legal action before shelter is given to her. One can appreciate the problem of the local authority in that without proof that the wife has grounds in law for leaving her husband it would not wish to become involved. However, if there are children involved it is much more likely that accommodation will be provided on a temporary basis to prevent their having to be taken into care. But the wife with no accommodation is often afraid, justifiably, that she will temporarily lose her children, and that her husband, having suitable accommodation, might well be granted custody of them. Alternatively, if the court hearing the custody dispute is aware of the fact that the wife is homeless and considers the husband unfit, then the children may be committed to the care of the local authority.

If a wife has been severely beaten it is obvious that she is justified in leaving the matrimonial home (and therefore not in desertion). Given this situation, one would expect a more liberal approach by the local authority in the matter of treating her as homeless; a more sympathetic – and realistic – approach would be to offer temporary accommodation but, if necessary, on condition that she take action within a specified time (and with advice) regarding legal separation, thus rendering her *legally* homeless. Alternatively the wife might apply for an injunction ordering the husband to vacate the matrimonial home – but this can be fraught with difficulty.

The vacation injunction

Again one returns to the statutes of 1925 and 1959 governing the power of the High Court and county courts respectively; again the judges have decided that the application for a vacation injunction must generally be ancillary to substantive matrimonial proceedings.

In the event of the wife being sole owner of the house, the courts will be prepared to order the husband to vacate it if necessary for the wife's protection. If the wife has some proprietary interest in the matrimonial home, for example as joint owner, then again she may be able to obtain an order evicting the husband. But in the situation where the wife has no proprietary interest whatsoever in the home, i.e. the husband is the sole owner, the judges have paid an inordinate amount of attention to the rights of the husband rather than the protection of the wife. The case law is far from consistent, but in extreme situations the courts are prepared to order the husband to vacate the home pending the hearing of the petition for divorce, etc.

The wife will always have the right to occupation of the matrimonial home during the subsistence of the marriage, and on divorce the court has power to make any order it thinks fit, including the transfer of property (including the matrimonial home) from one spouse to the other — but this is not usually the area of law with which the battered wife is immediately concerned. She does not wish to share the house with her spouse. She may or may not have decided on divorce, but in the interim she wants accommodation for herself and her children in the knowledge that her husband will not have the right to be on the premises.

Despite the judges' interpretation of the relevant statutes and their resultant restriction on their power to order the husband from the matrimonial home, they nevertheless insist (somewhat illogically) that where the safety of children is at stake, or where it is necessary in order to provide them with accommodation, they will have no hesitation in granting an injunction. They justify this by asserting that the protection of children is an inherent power vested in the courts — and does not therefore depend on there being any substantive proceedings! Laudable though this may be, either there is an unfettered power to grant injunctions or there is not; either the injunction application must be ancillary or it is capable of standing alone. In many cases the wife who has been subjected to persistent violence is just as vulnerable, just as much in need of the courts' protection, if not more so, than the children of the family, whose physical or mental health might be at serious risk if the father remains in the house.

Where the spouses share a council house or flat the judges have taken the view that they will not transfer the tenancy, since this would be a usurpation of the function of the housing authority. A substantial minority of local authorities will grant a joint tenancy to husband and wife, the majority still insisting that the husband be sole tenant. Where there is a joint tenancy the courts are more inclined to order the husband to vacate. If the husband is the sole tenant, then in exceptional circumstances he might be ordered to vacate — but the tenancy still remains in his name. A change is needed in the law in this area to bring it into line with the law regarding private tenancies. The latter can be transferred from one party to another on the termination of the marriage, the landlord being given an opportunity to be heard.

CONCLUSION

Violence by one or both parents towards the children of the family, and violence by one spouse towards the other, may or may not be on the increase — as with crime in general, the only indication of trends is the number of reported incidents. The result of an attack on an infant may be attributed to an accident; the battered wife may be too frightened to report the incidents or may see no practical alternative to suffering further attacks. Whatever the incidence of violence in the family, the attention focused on the battered wife and the battered baby is, healthily, increasing.

So far as the law is concerned, one can draw a distinction between its protective attitude, and the commensurately widespread legislation, so far as children are concerned. Here there are numerous provisions designed to prevent the occurrence of violence, in that interested persons can take prophylactic action. Distinguishable in law is the attitude towards the battered wife: here there is a dearth of protective law, in that the philosophy has been that the wife, being a person of the age of discretion, is able to protect herself and where necessary obtain legal redress just like any other person who is subjected to unlawful violence at the hands of another. Reform of the law is needed along the lines advocated in this chapter. It must be realised that the wife is often emotionally, financially and physically vulnerable and consequently must attract more protection under the law than a free agent who happens to be assaulted.

So far as the battered child is concerned, there is ample law to cover the majority of situations once they come to light. The lacuna in the social system is caused by insufficient collaboration and dissemination of information, coupled with inadequate facilities available to the interested bodies. So far as the battered wife is concerned, accommodation facilities are almost non-existent. Apart from criminal prosecutions, no action can be taken on her behalf, and she herself may be too distressed to be capable of rational thought and action. Finally, the law does not recognise her special position, and her particular need for temporary accommodation is not alleviated by the practice of housing authorities in granting tenancies to husbands and refusing to treat the battered wife as homeless unless she has proved her husband's cruelty in law by obtaining a separation order.

As always, it would be unrealistic to expect the law to provide a panacea: it cannot prevent violence, especially in such an emotional atmosphere as that which obtains in the nuclear family. It can merely provide a legal framework within which interested parties are given power to act. Where practicable it can impose duties rather than give powers, but ultimately the solution rests with those who have access to the family unit and who should realise that in a particular situation there is cause for concern.

Violence will not become obsolete, but at least the law can, and must, ensure that when it occurs and is detected its effects are mollified, even to the extent of making provision for society to accept responsibility for the welfare of the victim. So far as the battered wife is concerned, this does not yet appear to have become the accepted morality, and the law still insists on steps being taken towards the dissolution of the marriage before the plight of the wife is given full legal recognition.

ADDENDUM

Since this chapter was written new legislation has been enacted by Parliament. Schedule 3, paragraph 67, of the Children Act, 1975, came into force on 1 January 1976 and amends section 1(2) of the Children and Young Persons Act, 1969. The effect is to fill the gap in that Act mentioned on p. 91, and care proceedings *can* now be instituted in the situation described on that page.

Margaret Gregory *Psychologist*

6 BATTERED WIVES

This is what happened to Mary, aged thirty-five, with three daughters of one, four and seven years old. 'He had been in a filthy temper when he came home from work, then he went out and came back at half past eleven. The girls were asleep, but he woke them up, yelling 'Are those kids still here?' I locked the door of the back bedroom to keep the younger two safe, but he attacked me, thumping me and putting a knitting needle through my arm. Somehow – I don't quite remember when – I rang the police, but they said they couldn't do anything. The seven-year-old girl tried to protect me and she was hit too. He threw the rocking horse through the back window. I got myself into the back bedroom with the children and locked the door. A neighbour, an off-duty police sergeant, who must have heard the screaming, got us out down a ladder. We stayed at his house overnight and then were taken to a hostel thirty miles away.'

This incident, the last of many, took place in a green and leafy suburb. The husband was not charged with wounding his wife, though he had previously been convicted after stringing her up with light flex and so damaging her larynx that she had to be fed through a tube. The hospital had given evidence, and he had been fined £2. The house belonged to the wife, but he stayed there for some weeks and damaged it to the value of £700. When the divorce came to court he was at first denied access to the children, following evidence from the NSPCC, but was later allowed two hours' a week access. Mary was offered the chance to build a new life for herself and her children in America, but the husband exercised his paternal rights and would not allow the children to leave the country, though he has failed to pay the maintenance the court ordered.

At the time of the divorce the barrister said, 'A man like this is going to harrass you and these children for a very long time. I am going to do everything in my power to get you and the children out of the country.' The court would not agree to it, and a man who had not cared for his children or paid for their maintenance retained his paternal rights without having to show any sense of responsibility.

This is just one woman's case, but it contains many elements which are repeated thousands of times annually. For many years the police, the courts and social agencies have been unsuccessful in protecting women who

107

are being viciously assaulted by their husbands. The women themselves, lacking financial resources, housing and social support, cannot easily leave to establish a separate home for themselves and their children. In this chapter I want to examine some aspects of the problem and make some suggestions for more effective assistance. In writing I am very much aware of the limited nature of the evidence available. Three years ago the problem had yet to be brought to the attention of the public; two years ago the Chiswick refuge started to receive publicity, and since then, through press reports, feature articles and the establishment of many more refuges, it has become much more widely recognised.[1]

In what follows I have not drawn any distinction between the status of legal wife and common law wife. Other than in the matrimonial court, both have similar problems and both are equally in need of support.

EVIDENCE

Definition. Gayford[2] defines a battered woman as one 'who has received deliberate, severe and repeated physical injury from her husband . . . . At the very least this involves punching with the closed fist, at the worst attacks with broken bottles, knives and shootings.'

Extent. There has not been any definitive survey, if one is possible. Marsden and Owens,[3] through advertisements in the press and agency referrals, tried to contact as many battered women as possible in Colchester (population 72,000). Thirty-five women made contact, respresenting an incidence of 1 : 500 marriages, but after considering reports from doctors and solicitors of women who were not willing to be referred they estimated that the true incidence was likely to be 1 : 200 or even 1 : 100 marriages.

Some Citizens' Advice Bureaux have counted how many of their clients complained of marital violence when coming for help.[4] In 1972–73 seventy-one bureaux reported 3,150 enquiries from battered wives; in one year one bureau serving an area of 120,000 people reported seventy-one cases, of whom a third showed evidence of the violence at the time of the enquiry. Recently Salford City Citizens' Advice Bureau had twenty-six such enquiries in six weeks, and Leeds Samaritans report that 3 per cent of their clients are battered wives. Extrapolations from the CAB figures by Jack Ashley, MP, suggest a national incidence of between 20,000 and 50,000 cases a year.[5] Thus in a town with a population of 100,000 there are likely to be over 100 women asking some agency for other than medical help each year.

Types of violence and injury. Gayford interviewed 100 women, mainly from the Chiswick refuge, and found that all the women had been bruised; in forty-four cases there had been lacerations, seventeen of them caused by a sharp instrument; fifty-nine women had been repeatedly kicked; in forty-two cases some form of weapon had been used, such as a belt or broken bottle; there had been nineteen strangulation attempts and there were also burns and scalds. (Attacks with knives and guns are also known.) The type of injury suffered in these attacks is often severe. The bruises are a good deal worse than those which would result from walking into a door, a cupboard or a lamp post. One woman came to our Manchester refuge so badly bruised that there was no part of her face which was not purple and swollen. Other men direct their attacks on the body, aiming at breasts, abdomen or spine, so as to inflict the maximum pain while leaving no sign of injury when the woman is dressed. Gayford reported that thirty-four women had fractures, four had dislocations, nine had been taken to hospital unconscious, two received retinal damage and two suffered brain injury. Miscarriages caused by violence have been reported in most refuges, and quite a number of women report that their husband's violence increased when they were pregnant. Erin Pizzey is disturbed by the frequency with which women coming to Chiswick have handicapped children, and it is possible that a number of children are born damaged as a result of their father's violence.

It is sometimes asked why the woman does not hit back and defend herself. Some do, but few women are as strong as the average man; most have very strong inhibitions against being physically violent and little if any experience of fighting. For the wife to respond with violence would in most cases probably make an already difficult situation worse.

Murder. The criminal statistics published each year by the Home Office give the sex and age groupings of homicide victims, and show in a separate table the relationship of victim to suspect. This table does not distinguish between male and female spouse, but in 1973, out of 465 cases of homicide, there were ninety-seven in which a person met his or her death at the hands of the spouse or cohabitee.

In 1969 two studies of homicide were published: *Murder 1957–68,* by Gibson and Klein,[6] of the Home Office Statistical Unit, and *Criminal Homicide in England and Wales, 1957–68*[7] by the Legal Research Unit, Bedford College, London. Both set out to examine the effects, if any, on murder rates of changes in the law on capital punishment in 1957 and 1965. Neither gives the number of women who were killed by their husband, but both contain information which allows the figure to be estimated.

In cases of homicide there are several possible verdicts — murder and three categories of manslaughter. There are also cases where the suspect is not tried because he committed suicide or was found unfit to plead. The categories of manslaughter are: common law manslaughter; section 2 manslaughter, where the accused is found guilty but the charge is reduced from murder after consideration of his mental condition; and section 3 manslaughter, where the charge is reduced because of provocation by the victim. Gibson and Klein group together section 2 manslaughter, suicide and 'unfit to plead' cases as 'abnormal murder'. Other cases where the verdict was murder are classed as 'normal murder', for although the accused may have been suffering from some psychiatric condition it was not of a nature to impair his legal responsibility.

Gibson and Klein report separately the murders of husbands and wives. During the twelve-year period of their study 103 women were murdered by their husband or cohabitee, and eight men were murdered by their legal or common law wives. The information given for manslaughter and suspected suicide victims does not separate husbands from wives, but since 593 women were victims of abnormal murder, as against 190 men, and in 372 cases the victim in abnormal murder was the spouse of the suspect, it appears likely that an additional 270 to 300 women were killed by their spouse.

The Bedford College study reports on the third group, section 3 manslaughter with provocation. There were 194 such cases. Ninety-four per cent of the assailants were men, and their victims were men and women equally. In half the cases the victim was a member of the same family, but since the juries concerned did not accept provocation by children as grounds for amending the verdict it appears probable that a high proportion of women victims were the wife of the assailant, perhaps another sixty to seventy cases in twelve years. Over the whole twelve-year period it is likely that about 450 women were killed by their husband or cohabitee, i.e. nearly forty a year. The Bedford College study examined a 10 per cent sample of all offences in more detail. Of 177 cases in this sample, forty-three involved a man murdering his wife, cohabitee or fiancee; only four involved a woman murdering her husband, cohabitee or fiance. As this was a 10 per cent sample, the number over the whole period would be about 430 women killed, which is very close to the other estimate, although it excludes cases in which the suspect committed suicide. Both estimates suggest that over the period of the study about forty women a year were killed by their husbands.

Scott[8] reported in 1974 on forty men held in Brixton prison on suspicion of having murdered or attempted to murder their wives.

Fourteen of them had a long history of marital violence, and in six more cases the offence was preceded by a shorter but nevertheless severe period of violence. The implication is that the fatal offence could have been foreseen. It suggests that twenty murders a year might be prevented if there was at least somewhere women could go for safety, or if men who seriously assault their wives were apprehended and, when appropriate, given a custodial sentence or required to receive medical treatment.

Since 1968 the annual number of homicides has increased, and in 1973 there were ninety-seven cases involving the spouse. If the proportions have remained the same over the last ten years the number of lives which could be saved in one year may be over thirty. The study by Faulk[9] in 1974 supports this. He interviewed twenty-three men remanded in custody for seriously assaulting their wives, and also used information from prison records, though the wives, who in fifteen cases were apparently still alive, were not interviewed. In eight cases the men had been charged with murder, in nine cases with attempted murder, and in six with grievous or actual bodily harm or wounding. Half the men had no previous conviction, but 75 per cent had behaved in a threatening manner or had assaulted their wives before the attack which led to their remand. This warning was brought to the attention of the police in eight cases, and in one case to a doctor, but in seven cases only the victim was aware of the preceding violence. Faulk appears concerned that seven women did not report the warning incident, but the failure of the police to protect the eight who did may make their reticence less surprising.

The children. In at least half the families one or more of the children had been involved in the violence. Sometimes they were attacked when they were trying to protect their mother or when they were going for help; at other times the father or occasionally the mother punished them more severely than was reasonable.

Scott[10] reports on two studies of battered babies, one by Dr Selwyn Smith and one by himself, in which it appears that in a quarter of the cases the husband battered the wife. Often it was the husband who battered the baby. In other instances the wife passed on to the child some of the violence she had received herself.

There are several reports of the father interfering with his daughter sexually, and this is often the final straw that persuades a woman to leave. Virkkunen,[11] reporting on incest offences and alcoholism, found that aggressive behaviour was shown by 87 per cent of alcoholics and by 21 per cent of non-alcoholics convicted of incest.

In the refuges many children are found to be disturbed; the long-

standing troubles at home may be heightened by the sudden move. The
children in Marsden's community study do not appear to have been as
badly affected, but five were showing clear signs of disturbance. In the
families in the refuges bed-wetting is so common as to be normal, even by
children approaching their teens. Girls are often withdrawn and fearful.
Boys often reproduce aggressively the patterns of male behaviour they
have experienced at home. Some children who have been firmly repressed
later explode into a frenzy of attention-seeking behaviour.

Social background. Information about the social background and
characteristics of battered women is incomplete, but useful details can be
obtained from the two published surveys by Gayford and by Marsden and
Owens. The Liverpool refuge has records of forty women who have stayed
there, and in Manchester the Shield refuge has records for eight.

Those who come to refuges are not necessarily typical of all battered
women who wish to leave home. Many of them have tried to leave before
but had to return, often because of lack of resources. In other cases the
strain of living with relatives or friends in overcrowded accommodation,
and the disruption caused when an angry husband visits the house and
creates a disturbance, have enforced a return. Others go back because they
hope things will be better in future.

A middle class woman who decides to leave home usually has a better
chance of success, if she can overcome her sense of shame and guilt and
ask friends or relatives for help. She is more likely to know someone
with a house large enough to take her and the children. There will
usually be a telephone in case of emergency. She may have some money
in her own right, or a family able to help financially. She will probably
find it easier to obtain legal advice, though legal aid may well be more
difficult.

Interviewing in the general community, Marsden found that battered
women came from all social classes, except that labourers' wives were under-
represented in proportion to the national average. Over the last two years
I have come across twelve cases of battered wives not in refuges who had
a middle class background, and have met three of them. The husbands'
occupations included law, education, medicine, accountancy and
architecture, and many of the wives had been trained as teachers, nurses
or secretaries. I cannot wholly accept P. D. Scott's assertion that battering
is something which occurs mainly in social classes 4 and 5 alongside other
indices of social breakdown.

The main findings of the above surveys are summarised in table 6.1. In
addition a count made at Chiswick in January 1974 showed that during

Table 6.1

Summary of information from different surveys

	General population	Refuges			
		Chiswick –Gayford	Liverpool	'Shield' Manchester	Colchester –Marsden
Number:		100	40	8	19
Age at marriage:					
Wife	Mean 23 25% 16–20	Mean 20.3 60% 16–20	57% 16–20	All under 21	–
Husband	Mean 26–27	Mean 23.5	–	Four under 21	–
Conception:					
Pre-marital	Age of mother 70% 16–19	45	–	5	3
Extra-marital	19% 20–24	15	–	1	
Average family size	2.3	2.3*	2.9	3.3	–
Education after 15	25%. Percentage higher in London	30 women 18 men	–	2 women 1 man	–
Wife's family (No. with one or both parents absent at some time)	10% of one-parent families at any one time	35%	–	6	3
Violence in husband's childhood	–	51	–	7	6
Violence involved children	–	54	–	6	6

Continued on page 114

Table 6.1 (continued)

	General population	Refuges			
		Chiswick —Gayford	Liverpool	'Shield' Manchester	Colchester —Marsden
How soon after marriage violence started (years)	—	—	<1: 26 1–3 : 9 >3:3	<1:6 3:2	—
How long had they known each other before marriage? (months)	—	—	—	<6:1 6–12:2 >12:4	<6:5 6–12:5 >12:9

*Gayford reports the mean as 2.3, but later mentions the figure of 315 children.

Source. The general population statistics are taken from the following HMSO publications: 1961 census, education tables, published 1966; 1969 *Statistical Review* for England and Wales (births); 1973 *Social Trends,* No. 4 (age of marriage). The age groupings and presentation of information varied between surveys and some approximations have been necessary to facilitate comparisons.

the previous six months the refuge had sheltered 201 women (192 of them mothers of children) and 452 children. At least seven mothers were pregnant, and seven children were known to be in care. Of the 201 women, 150 came from London, twenty from the home counties, and the rest from all other areas of the British Isles.

It can be seen from the table that the women's level of education is very similar to that of the general population, that of the men probably slightly lower. The average number of children per family is similar to or slightly above the norm. There are two areas where the battered women do differ from the general population. They and their husbands tended to marry at a considerably younger age — at least three years earlier, on average — and the women from Chiswick and Manchester had often come from a one-parent family. The rate of pre-marital conception is normal for the age of marriage. The reasons for the absence of a parent varied considerably, death, illegitimacy and marital breakdown all being involved. However, most of the women did not consider they had had an unhappy or disturbed childhood, and in the Colchester sample the proportion with one parent absent is about the national average. It may be that the absence of a parent was a factor leading to early marriage in order to replace a home which had been lost or was recognised as incomplete.

Twenty-three of the women from Chiswick and one from Manchester had been exposed to family violence in their childhood, but for the husbands the rate of reported exposure to family violence was much higher, suggesting a marked familial pattern which will persist through several generations. 'He told me I ought to consider myself lucky I only had four children and was only beat up every two weeks or so, for his mum had eight children and was beat up every night.'

Most of the women reported that violence started early in marriage, often within a few weeks. While some knew before marriage that he could be violent, most had not recognised the trait in their future husband.[12] The early onset of violence suggests that this is a characteristic of the man rather than of the woman, in that very little time had elapsed for tensions to build up. Moreover very few men refrained from or reduced the level of violence when their wife was pregnant, and several women reported that it was worse at this time. Many women also report extreme sexual jealousy without any cause in terms of their own behaviour.[13]

Gayford also collected information on the behaviour of the woman's father and husband. Whereas twenty-seven of the fathers had drinking problems, this appeared to be true of seventy-four of the husbands. Four fathers gambled heavily, as did forty-four of the husbands. The husbands were three times more likely to be unemployed, and averaged slightly lower occupational status. Ten of the fathers, but over fifty of the husbands, had criminal records. The Shield hostel has no information about the fathers' record, but six of the eight husbands are reported as drinking heavily and assaulting their wives afterwards. The same six also have criminal records and a poor history of employment. Associated problems seem to have affected at least four men in the Colchester study.

Gayford gives some cultural information for his sample. He found that 66 per cent of the Chiswick women were British, as were 56 per cent of their husbands. The main immigrant groups were Irish and West Indian. Asian women and their husbands were under-represented, but otherwise the women appear to mirror the cosmopolitan character of London. Workers with the Community Relations Council in Manchester have found that this is a problem for some Asian women, and that such women often have great difficulty in approaching English institutions for help. Many Asians are unfamiliar with the social organisations of the host country and have difficulty in speaking English. The tradition of male dominance is very strong in some communities; it is often reinforced by the husband's relations, whose household the wife may have joined. Wife battering is a problem which occurs in most, perhaps all, social and ethnic groups in England and other countries. There is no definite evidence to suggest that it is more or less prevalent in any particular community, though there may well be such differences.

PROBLEMS FACED BY WOMEN

The law. This section is not a legal discussion, but looks at the law from the woman's point of view.[14] The legal position is complicated, so she will almost certainly require a solicitor and legal aid. Preliminary advice and a list of solicitors are available from the Citizens' Advice Bureaux. When a woman has been battered and does not wish to tolerate further violence she is faced with making a number of decisions affecting her future. Her first wish is usually to use the law to secure protection for herself and her children. In theory she can sue her husband for common law assault or possibly for one of the more serious categories of assault. The case will not be heard for some weeks, and it is necessary to have somewhere to live during that time. The case will be heard in the magistrates' court and is unlikely to be sent to a higher court. The sentence will probably be a fine or a conditional discharge. If the police have decided to charge the husband they may arrest him, and if when he appears in the magistrates' court the case is not to be heard immediately the wife should consider with her solicitor whether she will be safe if he is granted bail.

At present, however, criminal law prosecutions for marital assaults are infrequent, and a woman has to use the civil law. This usually means applying for a separation or a divorce. If she fears a repetition of the assaults she can apply to the county court for an injunction, which will usually forbid her husband to molest her or the children. In an emergency a good solicitor can get one in three or four days. It may also be possible to obtain an injunction requiring him to leave the family home, though this is difficult to do quickly, as the courts tend to consider that 'an Englishman's home is his castle', and give the man generous opportunities to defend himself.

A woman applying for an injunction is always in a stronger position if she has affidavits – sworn statements from one or more witnesses to support her case. These statements can be from friends or relatives to whom she has turned for help, or from hospitals or doctors who have provided treatment. One difficulty with an injunction is that it must be related to another legal action, usually a petition for divorce or separation, though in some cases it could be action for trespass or damages. However, starting divorce or separation proceedings does not commit the woman to completing them if the circumstances should change.

Another difficulty is that if the injunction is broken the woman has then to return to the court and complain before the court will take action. Breach of injunction is not a criminal offence, and it is the court bailiffs

who have the duty of apprehending the offender, not the police. I know
of one case where the man contrived to avoid being served with the
warrant for breach of injunction for six months, continuing all the time
to commit further breaches. Nevertheless the injunction can be helpful as
many men will respect the court order, and if the police are called to a
man who is breaking the injunction they are more likely to take seriously
any other offence he has committed and remove him. However, when a
man is imprisoned for contempt of court following a breach of injunction,
the woman does not know for how long this will be, since he may be
considered to have purged his contempt after a few days, so putting her at
risk again.

Many women have been shocked to discover how little protection the
courts have offered them. Sentences for assaults within the family are often
much lighter than they would be for similar assaults outside, as the courts
do not relish putting a man in prison for a long time if there is any
possibility he may have been provoked. The women who have been
battered may sympathise with this – 'What he needs is help, not punishment' – but they want safety for themselves. When a violent husband
comes out of prison or is divorced he often puts considerable pressure on
his former wife to accept him back, as he has nowhere else to go. Very
little help is available for the men concerned, though many are in need
of it. Some form of hostel where they could be required to live while
learning a new pattern of life would be valuable.

The police. It has proved very difficult to discover exactly what police
powers are in 'domestic cases'. The police have a duty to investigate all
complaints and should see the complainant, but the investigation is often
cursory. Many policemen clearly feel that most domestic disputes are
short-lived and are not usually serious. To quote a police community
relations officer, 'We step out rather quickly. Unless there is a serious
injury we suggest they take their own recourse. Police experience is that
next morning both husband and wife combine against the police, so we
try for first aid to stop a breach of the peace. When there are more
serious injuries the criminal code applies.' However, it is quite clear from
reports from many parts of the country that the police are failing to use
the criminal law in cases where the assault has occasioned clear injury
which would have led to charges of grievous or actual bodily harm in
any other circumstances.

Having left her husband because of violence, Mrs A. returned home, at
a time when she expected him to be out, to collect clothes for the baby.
But her husband was in, and when he realised she did not intend to stay

he started to attack her. Followed by her husband, she ran out of the house. He punched her in the face and knocked her to the ground, then turned his anger against the pram. Mrs A. ran, bleeding from nose and mouth, to ask a passing policeman for help. In front of her husband the policeman told her to get back into the house and fight there or *she* would be arrested for breach of the peace!

Is it surprising that women feel they often have no alternative but to return to the violent husband?

Mrs B., who was staying in a refuge, returned home to collect clothes. Those in the refuge felt she had been away a long time and asked the police to investigate. The police went to the house and witnessed the assault, being at the house for twenty minutes, during which time Mr B. continued to strike his wife. They made no attempt to restrain him. After twenty minutes Mrs B. was able to run out of the house, bleeding from nose and mouth and with a cut above her eye, and run to the police station. The desk sergeant said, 'We are not supposed to get involved in domestic cases,' and the police refused to prosecute. Mrs B. suffered a broken nose, the cut above her eye required four stitches, and she had two black eyes, and multiple and severe bruising of the body, legs and neck. Later her husband attacked her again, breaking three ribs. Again the police refused to charge him, and charges for assault were brought by Mrs B. herself. He was fined £25 on each count.

A much less severe case, which illustrates the unhelpful attitude women so frequently encounter: 'My daughter went out to the phone. The police came but said they could not interfere in a domestic case. I had a black eye, and I asked them to take me and the children up to my sister's, about a mile away, but they said they did not run a taxi service.' On another occasion the blow to the wife's eye caused a haemorrhage requiring two days' in-patient treatment and daily out-patient visits for over two weeks. On other occasions he dragged her downstairs, banging her head and back. In countless incidents of this type the police attitude, by apparently in failing to condemn, effectively condones and even encourages the man's belief that he can behave as he sees fit in his own home.

There are cases where men have been prosecuted for assaulting their wives, but they seem to be infrequent and to have involved the use of a weapon and/or serious injury such as a fractured skull. There are other instances where the police have been prepared to prosecute, but when the case came to be heard the woman was unwilling to give evidence, often because of threats of further violence from her husband. The police complain of the time it takes to prepare a case only to have the woman back down. Clearly this happens, but in other types of criminal assault the victim does not have to live in the same house as the assailant until the case has been heard.

The police frequently advise women of their right to take out a summons for common law assault, yet again the same difficulty arises. The woman who wishes to take out a summons will have to find alternative accommodation until such time as the case is heard – usually six weeks – and, unless the sentence is custodial, for some time after the case. If a person is assaulted and given a black eye by someone other than the spouse the police will normally charge the assailant themselves. At present their practice means that a woman who is assaulted by her husband receives little protection. The police rarely arrest, nor, apparently, do they often rebuke the man verbally, warn him, or invite him to 'Come down to the station and have a talk about it' – all tactics they commonly use in cases where the offender is not necessarily charged.

Housing. This is a major problem for battered women. They have usually been adequately housed but, as with the majority of the population, the home is usually in the husband's name. Occasionally the tenancy or ownership is the woman's, but either way it is the woman, usually accompanied by the children, who has to leave. There is an immediate need for a refuge where she and the children will be safe and she can consider her future. However, many local authorities still refuse to recognise violence as a cause of homelessness, and may refuse to take even the obviously bruised woman into emergency accommodation, claiming that she has a home to go to.

If the wife decides to separate she may wish to be rehoused some distance away so as to be safe, or she may want to return to the neighbourhood she knows. After a separation order local authorities will usually be willing to grant the tenancy to the wife if she has custody of the children, but if the husband is unwilling to leave they tend to put the onus of evicting him on the woman. In any event, if the husband does not co-operate it may be months before she can repossess the home, either for her own use or as an exchange tenancy, and in this time he may well have damaged it or disposed of the furniture. After a divorce the court may award the woman the right to occupy the family dwelling, but for legal reasons she may not be able to sell it in order to move to a safer place. When the human relationship side of marriage has failed so completely the physical side – the house and furniture – may become even more important, and the distress caused by having to leave a home created and furnished with devotion can be considerable.

Financial problems. Battered women who leave home are a particularly vulnerable group within a disadvantaged section of society — one-parent families. Their financial difficulties often start before separation, are acute when they leave, and often continue for as long as they have dependent children.

Marital violence occurs in all social classes, but since many husbands are heavy drinkers and gamblers the family is often worse off than need be. The wife may have had to manage on a limited budget, and will rarely have much money of her own. This makes it difficult to leave. The cost of transport for a woman and perhaps three or four children has to be found. If staying with friends, she cannot eat their food as well as occupy their house. If she can go on working this may provide sufficient income; if not she has to turn to Social Security.

Having to apply for Social Security benefit is an unhappy experience for anyone, and for a woman as humiliated and frightened as many battered wives are it is particularly so. If she has private accommodation she will have to prove that she has left her husband, explain why, and plead with the official not to reveal her address when asking the husband for his 'liable relatives' contribution.

If she has not yet started legal proceedings for divorce or separation, benefit may be refused. When refuges first opened the women in them often had difficulties of this nature, but through regional and national co-operation with the DHSS working arrangements have been evolved which avoid some of the most difficult situations. In addition to the weekly problem of paying rent and feeding the children, a woman who has had to leave home may be very short of clothes for herself and the children, and unable to go back to collect them. In such circumstances application has to be made to DHSS for a 'special needs' grant to help bridge the gap.

In the longer term the family is likely to be in financial difficulties. Few husbands can be relied upon to pay maintenance regularly, while the Finer report[16] on one-parent families shows how the low level of women's earnings makes it difficult for most women with children to earn appreciably more than their Social Security entitlement. Part-time work for more than a few hours a week is precluded by the earnings limit, which means that the woman loses in benefit the equivalent of all earnings over £4. Part-time work is, however, valuable in providing social contact for a woman who may otherwise be very isolated, and in equipping her for more responsible full-time employment when the children are older. Employment also provides the insurance stamps which are necessary to qualify for retirement pension and other benefits in her own right.

A woman on Social Security may have her order book withdrawn quite suddenly, and this can leave her without money for several weeks. One ground for withdrawal is actual or suspected cohabitation. The stringency with which the rule is applied in some areas can make it very difficult for a woman to establish a friendship with a man which might lead to remarriage and a new life for the family.

DISCUSSION

Is there a psychopathology? Those of us concerned with refuges have come to know the women personally and have also gathered detailed information from them through questionnaires. Scott and Faulk have reported on men in prison, but there is no study of violent husbands who have not been imprisoned, although some of the questionnaires ask the women to describe their husband's background and behaviour. From all these sources of information certain patterns emerge.

The women are rarely psychiatrically ill, though many, understandably anxious and depressed, are taking prescribed drugs to alleviate the condition. Some will have taken an overdose, but the 'cry for help' has often gone unheeded in that they were returned to the same domestic situation that had precipitated it. Within the refuges there have, of course, been some difficulties in the relationship between the women themselves and their children: it is not easy to share overcrowded accommodation with others for several months without friction. However, it is rare for tension to express itself in physical violence between the women or directed at the children. Rather they work together and support each other through a stressful time. Psychiatric abnormality or personality disorder in the women does not, therefore, appear to be a reasonable explanation of their husbands' violence. This is not to claim that all are totally conciliatory and perfect housekeepers, just that they are representative.

The picture which emerges of the husbands is very different. Heavy drinking, gambling, unemployment and convictions for other offences are all commonly reported, and many of them come from homes which were themselves violent. In some cases the violence develops as part of a psychiatric breakdown after a previously normal life, but more often it begins soon after marriage and persists. This suggests a pattern of behaviour learnt in childhood. Such men appear to have a low 'flash point' when irritated and to lack alternative defence mechanisms or displacement activities for coping with difficulties. Within the home most people behave in a less controlled manner than outside, and just as a normal child will continue to have tantrums at home for some time after learning that this is not the way to behave elsewhere, so the violent husband may behave like an overgrown child at home.

Some husbands are very jealous with little or no cause, distrusting every move their wife makes and imputing quite unjustifiable relationships. It may be quite difficult to define when the jealousy is delusional and when just over-suspicious, but many extreme cases have been reported. This delusional jealousy is particularly dangerous for the woman, since rational argument is not possible.

Attitudes of society. There are many attitudes and assumptions in our society which can serve to support violent husbands. 'An English*man's* home is *his* castle.' 'She must have done something to deserve it.' 'She must get something out of it.' Often emphasis is placed upon a man's rights but upon the woman's duties. In many situations a married woman's status is only that of her husband's wife, for example in not being allowed to fill in her own income tax return, or in the formal mode of address as 'Mrs John Smith'. The attitudes reflected in these and similar customs help to emphasise her dependence and make it more difficult for her to face life on her own.

Social agencies have a long tradition of supporting the family unity and the 'sanctity of marriage'. This has frequently led to women being given quite unrealistic advice to 'try again for his sake', or for the sake of the children, even in cases where the violence has lasted for ten years or more. Such advice can be justified only if the man is clearly willing to accept help in order to change his behaviour substantially. Promising not to drink so much is less effective than becoming an active member of Alcoholics Anonymous. Children are not helped by growing up in a violent and fearful home; they have a better chance with one parent and no violence.

Refuges and Women's Aid. In 1971 a group of women came together in Chiswick to do something about rising prices. After a short while the London borough of Hounslow gave them the keys of a small and nearly derelict house awaiting demolition to use as an information advice centre. This was the start of Chiswick Women's Aid, and it rapidly became a centre for women needing help and advice on all manner of subjects. Quite soon the first battered wife came for help.

In other areas of Britain Women's Aid Centres were also being established, and they too were approached for help by women who had been turned away or ignored by other agencies. Gradually the nature of

the problem of marital violence became more widely known, and
estimates of its extent began to be made. Some statutory agencies which
had previously failed to respond became a little more generous, and
groups throughout Britain set about establishing refuges. By 1975
twenty-seven refuges were open and more planned. Many refuge groups
have joined the National Women's Aid Federation[15] to share experience
and co-ordinate publications and publicity. The groups establishing
refuges vary considerably. Many are closely connected with Women's
Liberation groups, others involve social workers, magistrates, Church
groups and members of other women's organisations. Some refuge support
groups consist of women only, others include men.

Very few refuges have a resident warden. None provides meals, as do
many local authority hostels. In all refuges the women care for their
own children and support each other in times of particular difficulty. The
intention is to encourage a self-governing community in which those whose
confidence has been badly shaken can recover their self-respect and
ability to cope. The support group provides some continuity of experience
in contacting other agencies, social service and housing departments,
solicitors and Social Security, as well as people to talk to when problems
threaten to become overwhelming. Some refuges have been able to employ
a worker to provide greater continuity of support than is possible from a
voluntary group alone.

The houses used as refuges vary considerably, from the large house at
Chiswick, which has taken seventy people, to four-room cottages with an
outside w.c. Some refuges started as squats in empty property to meet a
particular emergency. Others were carefully planned and negotiated, and
the property eventually provided by the local authority or a commercial
firm. Furnishings have usually been scrounged, and the standards of
physical comfort are often low because of this and because of the
overcrowding. Some groups, supported by their local authority, have
obtained urban aid grants from the Home Office, so enabling them to
employ workers and play leaders for the children.

Though attitudes and philosophy vary from group to group, the
overall approach is that the refuge gives a woman the right to decide her
own future. She is not forced to remain in a dangerous marriage for lack
of an alternative, but neither is she committed to a divorce as soon as she
arrives. The refuge provides a safe haven in which she can review her
position and talk it over with others who understand the problems.
Perhaps half the women coming to refuges decide to separate, the others
to go home and try to rebuild their marriage. Some of these come back
for a second or third stay; for others the reconciliation succeeds. The

central philosophy is a recognition of the woman's right to decide her future, whereas traditional marriage counselling has too often emphasised the duty of keeping the family together, so that women have been advised to return to an appalling situation. In the refuge she should be supported in whatever decision she makes. If help is wanted to rebuild a marriage, it will be obtained if possible, as will legal advice and contact with community support groups for those who choose to end the marriage.

RECOMMENDATIONS

Finance. The Finer report[16] on one-parent families discusses their financial position and suggests a 'guaranteed maintenance allowance' for all such families, which would integrate the 'special needs' allowances with the general Social Security benefit and recognise that extra expenses are incurred by a one-parent family. It would be assessed for three months at a time, the adult portion of the allowance being subject to a 50 per cent taper in respect of other earnings but the children's portion not being affected. Short-term cohabitation would not affect the allowance, but longer relationships and remarriage would end the entitlement.

This guaranteed maintenance allowance would be of considerable help to long-term one-parent families, but it does nothing for them at the time of crisis, since it would not be available until six months after the break-down. The allowance would be calculated in association with the system of tax credits recommended in a Green Paper of October 1972. I believe that a more effective way of helping all low-income families would be to provide a larger family allowance, paid, as now, to the mother or caring parent at a post office, and to abolish the child tax allowances. A guaranteed maintenance allowance in addition to this would, of course, be welcomed.

The present tax allowance of £240 per year for a child under eleven is of no value to the family whose income is below the tax limits. A family paying tax at the standard rate saves £80 per child per year, while a family with an income of £16,000 and a marginal tax rate of 68 per cent saves £163 per child per year. If a family allowance of £3 a week for each child, including the first, were paid to all families, the mother would have a useful though still inadequate source of income on which she could draw in emergencies. The amount of this allowance should be linked to the cost of living and reviewed regularly, like other pensions. Where claimants are receiving Social Security the increased family allowance should not be wholly offset by reducing the Social Security benefit. Such a change would award a significant income to the woman 'as of right'; it would not have to be specially applied for at a time of crisis, and would not be lost if she worked, cohabited or remarried. It would assist all low-income families and, for the better off, would be balanced by the loss of tax allowances.

The report makes many detailed and sensible recommendations for assisting one-parent families in addition to the guaranteed maintenance allowance. In particular it recommends that for income tax purposes the single parent should be awarded the increased personal allowance of the married man. The 1975 budget has taken some steps to assist single-parent families, but they are as yet very limited ones.

As remarked earlier, there are a number of families in substantial rent arrears, often accumulated while the husband was receiving Social Security benefit but diverting much of the benefit from the home. I have encountered three cases where this happened and where, owing to earlier difficulties, the tenancy of the home was in the wife's name. It would appear right that under these circumstances she should be able to draw both the householder's and children's benefits, while the man draws only his personal allowance.

The law. The introduction of a 'family court' which would be responsible for all matters associated with the breakdown of marriage and the care of juveniles is recommended in the Finer report, where the procedures are discussed in some detail. This would greatly simplify the complexity of legal administration which at present confronts a battered woman and her legal advisers, who have not always been able to use the existing law effectively.

At present there is often little point in a woman bringing charges or giving evidence in criminal proceedings against her husband, because the sentence of the court may not afford her any protection. Penalties are often lighter than for non-marital assaults, and if the husband is fined it is the housekeeping or maintenance payments that suffer. The fine itself may exasperate him, producing further assaults. Sentencing policies should take into account the woman's need for safety and the possibility of helping the man as well as showing society's disapproval of his behaviour. The use of probation orders and probation hostels as an alternative to prison might be examined.

Injunctions are civil, not criminal, orders, but there are circumstances when they should be enforceable by the police, who are on duty at times when court bailiffs are not available.

Some policemen believe they have few rights in matrimonial disputes, though other officers and lawyers claim that the police have ample powers to protect battered women. I feel it is essential that the powers of the police should be clarified so that they feel able to arrest if there has been an assault of a type which would merit it outside the home. They would then be more likely to warn borderline cases rather than 'not interfere in domestic disputes'. This is not a demand for a prosecution every time the police are called in to a domestic dispute, but a request that, as agents of society, they should be conscious that violent behaviour is no more acceptable inside the home than outside.

Medical services. Often the medical services are the first to be approached because the woman needs treatment for injuries or because she is suffering from stress. It appears that both general practitioners and casualty departments treat the symptoms but usually make few enquiries as to their cause. Cuts are stitched, broken bones set, or a prescription for tranquillisers written, and the woman is returned to her dangerous home. Sometimes the woman visiting the casualty department will give a false and often inadequate explanation of her injuries. On other occasions she admits the cause, but if no further reference is made to it by the hospital her sense of isolation and shame is deepened. When a casualty department is treating a woman in this way it would help if someone, probably the casualty sister, tried to talk a little about what had happened, found out whether the patient would feel safer if she had alternative accommodation, or contacted a social worker for further discussion during the next few days. Above all, the hospital, like other social agencies, should recognise that when a woman has been assaulted and injured by her husband she is not bound to return to him but has the right to reconsider the future pattern of her life, and may choose independence.

Social services. Social workers have generally wished to support the family, and are often reluctant to assist a woman who wants to leave home. Their advice has frequently been to 'try again', and sometimes they have offered to take the children into care rather than assist them through the mother. This failure to provide effective help has, I believe, two main causes: lack of facilities for emergency housing and a lack of preparation in social work training. For a few years now, training courses have been helping them to recognise and handle cases of baby battering, but few social workers appear to have had much preparation or guidance for dealing with other forms of violence, particularly marital violence; nor is the latter mentioned in the literature of social work. This lack of preparation often leads workers to dismiss what some clients tell them as exaggerated, with a consequent failure to follow up the tentative indications provided by others.

As the extent of the problem becomes more widely recognised, Social Services Departments need to respond by providing refuges and support services themselves, or by assisting voluntary groups to do it. There is also a need for crisis centres where women can go just to talk over their problem. These too could be provided by voluntary groups if they were given some financial support.

Housing. The Finer report makes clear recommendations for the transfer of tenancy and occupation of the family home. They would allow the court to evict the husband and secure the wife's right to occupy it.

Local authorities should be obliged to accept marital violence as a *prima facie* cause of homelessness. When a local authority tenant wishes to move to another area for reasons of safety, the authority should assist the transfer. Similarly, when a tenant has to take refuge in another area there should be no loss of housing rights in the place of origin.

Research. At the beginning I emphasised the many uncertainties due to lack of information. Many refuges are collecting information from the women they shelter, and this will serve to provide a picture of the people who use refuges, their problems and the courses of action chosen. Often a refuge may wish to continue to provide support when a woman leaves, but shortage of resources makes this difficult and so limits the quality of follow-up data.

Perhaps the most valuable study would be a community survey seeking to define the extent and type of marital violence prevalent in the community, and in particular whether there are more than just a few marriages which have gone through a period of violence, such as those described earlier, and have later steadied down to non-violent and acceptable relationships. This is particularly important in view of the changes in police practice which are suggested. The police are reluctant to interfere in a situation which may be temporary, yet they know they are called to the same home time after time, year after year. The refuges know of violent marriages which lasted thirty years before the woman was able to leave, but no one can say how many marriages eventually calm down.

Psychiatric assessment of the men, and the development of ways of treating them, would also be of value. The greatest need, however, is to help some very disturbed children in such a way as to avoid a third generation of violence.

ACKNOWLEDGEMENTS

I should like to thank Erin Pizzey for helping me count cases in Chiswick, the Liverpool refuge for allowing me to quote from their records, Sue Marrs of Manchester, who tabulated the figures from Liverpool, and all the women in London, Liverpool and Manchester who have helped by filling in questionnaires.

NOTES

1 Erin Pizzey, *Scream Quietly or the Neighbours will Hear*, Penguin, 1974.
2 J. J. Gayford, 'Wife battering: a preliminary survey of 100 cases', *British Medical Journal*, vol. 1, No. 5951, p. 194, 25 January 1975.
3 D. Marsden and D. Owens, 'The Jekyll and Hyde marriages', *New Society*, vol. 32, No. 657, p. 333, 8 May 1975.
4 'Citizens' Advice Bureaux' experience of the problem of battered women', memorandum for the DHSS, National Citizens' Advice Bureaux Council, 26 Bedford Square, London W.C.1.
5 Jack Ashley, Report of House of Commons debate, Hansard, 17 July 1973, pp. 218–27.
6 E. Gibson and S. Klein, *Murder, 1957–68*, London, HMSO, 1969.
7 *Criminal Homicide in England and Wales, 1957–68*, interim report of the Homicide Research Project, Legal Research Unit, Department of Sociology, Bedford College, University of London.
8 P. D. Scott, 'Battered wives', *British Journal of Psychiatry*, vol. 125, 1974, p. 433.
9 M. Faulk, 'Men who assault their wives', *Medicine, Science and the Law*, vol. 14, 1974, p. 180.
10 P. D. Scott, 'Fatal battered baby cases', *Medicine, Science and the Law*, vol. 13, 1973, p. 197.
11 M. Virkkunen, 'Incest offences and alcoholism', *Medicine, Science and the Law*, vol. 14, 1974, p. 124.
12 'The first time he beat me was two weeks after we were married. He reckoned I hadn't cooked the cabbage right. I was so stunned I just went and walked round the park for hours. You see, I just did not know that things like this could happen.'
13 'If I went to the shops with the children and because the shops were crowded was longer than he thought I should have been, he would accuse me of having it off with a fellow. If I went across the road to talk to my friend he would say I was a lesbian.'
14 Tess Gill and Anna Coote, *Battered Women — How to use the Law*, Cobden Trust, 186 King's Cross Road, London WC1X 9DE; Anna Coote and Tess Gill, *Women's Rights: a Practical Guide*, Penguin, 1974.
15 *Battered Women Need Refuges*, report from the National Women's Aid Federation, 51 Chalcot Road, London N.W.1.
16 *Report of the Committee on One-parent Families* (the Finer report), London, HMSO, 1974.

7   POLICE INVOLVEMENT

The sacrificial lamb on the altar of social expediency – this is how one might describe the plight of victims of violence. Is our society guilty of concealing certain offences against children and women because it is merely more convenient on occasions to do so?

It is argued by some that in a violent society there should be a repressive agency; the aggressor should be restrained and the victim protected. The British police officer has an accepted place in society; his role is multifarious. To the overseas visitor he is 'wonderful'; to the criminal discovered he is 'Nemesis'; to the battered child he is a protector; to the assailant he poses a threat; but to the battered wife he may seem an idle bystander. Thus through different eyes the police are seen in diverse ways; as protectors of the weak to some or perhaps as persecutors of minority groups to others.

Each police officer is sworn to protect life and property and to preserve public tranquillity. The protection of life goes beyond mere restraint of physical violence and extends to what may be termed 'offenders against the person'. The law extends special protection to the more vulnerable or easily exploited groups of society, for instance children.

The police do not make the law, but have a duty to enforce it, whether they as individuals sympathise with all it decrees or not. Over the years there has been a growing recognition within the police service of social and psychological factors in many law-breaking situations, and this has influenced the development of the police role. It may be that we still have much to learn, but most officers like to believe that they act out their role not only with common sense but with humanity, both towards the victim and on many occasions towards the law-breaker too.

The role of the police is not punitive. Although we are the law enforcement agency, I personally consider the police force to be the primary social service in this country. Those of us who have spent a lifetime in the police service have been engaged many long hours dealing with calls for help in the social welfare field. Surveys reveal that most calls made to police stations are related to social problems, not law enforcement problems. Many social service agencies are now alive to the fact that social work is a round-the-clock business, and provision is made for a member of staff to be available out of office hours and at weekends. Indeed, it is at these times that most crises develop and the inadequate are subject to the gravest tensions and require emergency help. We have not yet, however, reached this state of Utopia in all areas.

What most of us are anxious to do is get to grips with problems and work as part of a team with members of other disciplines, so that the people who need help can benefit from our joint expertise. It must be pointed out, however, that there will be occasions when our points of view diverge and the police officer will believe that there should be a prosecution while the social worker will feel strongly that this course would be the worst possible thing for the offender and the family unit as a whole. We must by mutual trust overcome our differences. The police should realise that in many cases understanding and help will be more beneficial than a court appearance, while doctors, social workers and nurses should realise that at times court proceedings are not only necessary but desirable for all concerned.

When the police have information that an offence has been committed they should investigate it and present the relevant facts to a senior officer, who will decide what further action will be taken. An investigation does not always mean a prosecution. Senior police officers can and do make humane decisions daily.

Child abuse. Child beating is no new thing. Hogarth's seventeenth-century prints, in which the artist satirised the follies of his time, depict the careless, drunken parent exposing children to all kinds of danger. So we have gone on over the years, only recently recognising the extent of the problem of what is now politely termed 'non-accidental injury'. Many people refuse steadfastly to believe that parents will harm their own children, though research has shown that a large number of people are capable of hurting their young.

This is where, I believe, the training and the role of the police officer are so different from that of many other professions who train their members to question people in order to help them and so believe the answers to their questions. The police officer is trained to question the answers. If we believed everything said to us we would detect little crime. In spite of this somewhat sceptical attitude we are nevertheless skilled at talking to people in many walks of life, without condescension, hardness or brutality and – difficult though many find it to believe – we treat the majority of people with whom we have to deal comparatively kindly.

I think the police are aware that because a woman has given birth to a child she is not automatically endowed with maternal instincts and feeling, and that even people who feel great love for their offspring can at times be driven beyond the limits of their endurance. In recent years great strides have been made towards understanding the problem of child abuse. There is frequent consultation between various agencies concerned with child welfare (including the police) in order to benefit the child. There is still much to be done in the field of collaboration, and in many areas there remains a lack of trust. There is still the gravest suspicion on the part of other professions involved that the police will take all cases coming to their notice before the courts. I would stress again that chief officers give serious consideration to any representation made on behalf of any person by a doctor or social worker. However, we must accept that a person who may be in need of treatment which he will not accept on a voluntary basis may have to be taken before the court so as to be made the subject of a hospital order.

The practice in some police forces of using the police surgeon is a good one. It means that any child who has been injured can be examined by this doctor, who is not only skilled in giving evidence in court but is not close to the family, thus preserving the doctor–patient relationship of the family GP.

The current practice of having case conferences over suspect cases of child abuse is an excellent one, and I feel strongly that the police should always be represented, preferably by an officer of a rank senior enough to make a decision on the spot if necessary. We sometimes feel that we are called in only on the occasions when alarm is felt, and this can be too late.

Domestic disputes. Domestic disputes lead, by the order of human nature, to the aggressive traits of one or both partners coming to the fore and on many occasions resulting in attack and injury by one partner on the other. The *usual* pattern is attack by the husband on the wife, now known as wife battering. In this field the police service is often accused of not being active enough. It is remarked that police officers attend domestic disputes and do not do anything.

Wife battering is not some new social ill, but through the news media it has become a recognised problem in the world today. Its incidence may be slightly exaggerated by supporters of the Women's Liberation movement, who resent women being seen as sex symbols or chattels of men and tend to be extremist. Extremism is useful on occasions because it attracts attention to a cause and, because of this, action *may* follow.

Complaints are often made that police attending domestic disputes where the wife has been attacked take no official action. *The police are always bound by law and the laws of evidence.* In order to take the appropriate action, they, as prosecutors, must be able to produce the best evidence, and this is not always readily forthcoming.

It has been said that the man who beats his wife is not really conscious of his actions at the time. Many people feel that men who cannot express their feelings adequately in words resort to violence as their only means of self-expression. Whatever the shortcomings of these men, and whatever their need, the role of the police is to keep the peace and protect life and property. No matter what conclusion we reach about their aggression and the help and treatment needed by certain types of men, we are bound to do our duty and to take action *if we have proof of an offence*.

We need first of all a complainant, in addition to the necessary injury. To fulfil the first requirement it is essential that the prosecution have a witness who will testify as to how, why and where the injury occurred. One would think this was simple, yet it is amazing that, however many hundred calls to domestic disputes are answered by the police, and however many wives have sustained injury, few are eventually prepared to go into the witness box at court and give the necessary evidence.

With regard to the degree of assault, ranging from common assault to the very serious crime of wounding with intent, it is necessary to prove injury. Frequently the police are called to scenes of domestic dispute and allegations of assault are made. With many of these alleged assaults there is no obvious sign of injury and we therefore have to rely on the word of the complainant. This lack of direct evidence (e.g. signs of injury are lacking) makes the offence one of common assault, which is the least serious of this group of offences. A definition of assault under common law is 'the intent or offer or threat by force or violence to do harm to another' and the punishment for it is laid down in section 42 of the Offences against the Person Act, 1861.[1]

Proceedings under this section *must* be taken by the aggrieved person. The aggrieved person must lay an information before a Justice on his or her own behalf against the offender. The police do not assume this responsibility unless the complainant is old and infirm, and is not a free agent but under the control of the person committing the assault. Many people would here say that a married woman is under the control of her husband and not a free agent, and therefore the police should act for her.

It has, however, been recognised in law for many centuries that the sanctity of marriage is something special. Until recent times a wife was seen as a chattel of her husband and had no real rights. In recent years it has become obvious to the writer, through years of police experience as a practical officer, that however often one says to a wife, 'Your rights are . . .' she will invariably be re-influenced by her husband and refuse to give the necessary evidence. Whether this is basically due to personal fear or to an essentially sexual attraction and influence, or to fear for the children of the union, it is difficult to determine. I only know how frustrating it is for a police officer who has taken much care and trouble in the preparation of the presentation of the case at court to be let down because his principal witness has had 'second thoughts'. If positive action is desirable when injury has been caused, quite often severe injury, we must overcome the problem of the wife who is unwilling to give evidence. Often her decision not to do so is made at the last minute, either as a result of reconciliation or perhaps through fear of retribution. From a practical viewpoint it would appear better to charge the husband and keep him in custody, rather than to follow the practice in some few police areas where the husband is reported for summons, thus giving him time to influence his wife. If some aggressive husbands are, by these means, kept away from the matrimonial home, more wives may be prepared to give the relevant evidence.

In large cities where police officers are called to the scenes of many incidents and assaults in one tour of duty, one would find the practice of arrest and charge, with appearances at court the next morning, to be prevalent. In the more rural areas the system often adopted is to report the offender and summons him to appear before court at a later date.

It has recently been queried whether the police should be involved in domestic matters. Are we the correct agency to deal with domestic disputes? If not, how can an effective filter operate to ensure that our tasks of crime prevention and detection are maintained? On this point I would reiterate that we are the sole agency available twenty-four hours a day, seven days a week, to enter into any situation, garbed with the cloak of authority, to sift and assess the gravity of each occurrence. (As I write, it is a bank holiday. I know the colleagues of my profession are on duty and available to arrive within minutes of any summons for help. How many other agencies concerned with the welfare of our fellow men are similarly geared?)

Many domestic disputes, quite often reported initially as unimportant, turn out to be cases of serious wounding, manslaughter, even murder, and therefore the police service, trained to meet these emergencies, is the obvious, only agency to attend in the first instance. It would, however, be useful to have the back-up support of other services at all times to pass on those cases which are purely social problems and which need the understanding and expertise of people highly trained in their field.

There is a feeling that social workers often obtain first-hand information that assaults, woundings and more serious offences have been committed. This information is concealed, perhaps through ignorance of the law, in the belief that the loyalty of the social worker should rest entirely with the client. Information about offences may come to the notice of social workers in the first instance, and it would be well for all to remember that they have a moral duty to report any such offence to the police.

It must be admitted that in cases of minor assault the police are on occasions too reluctant to take action. This, however, is due to the reasons mentioned above — that the heavily dramatic atmosphere prevailing, especially when there is little evidence of injury, is quickly dissipated and husband and wife are reconciled; if not, the wife can take her own action for the offence of common assault.

There would seem to be good reason for using the provisions of the Criminal Evidence Act, 1898, and common law regarding the competency and compellability of a spouse's evidence more frequently. In cases of actual physical injury on the one by the other a wife is both competent and compellable by law to give evidence. As we have seen, wives are too often persuaded not to pursue complaints. The answer would seem to be to charge the husband as opposed to reporting him for summons. In the first case he would be removed at once and placed in custody, whereas in the second there is the disadvantage of the man being left at home. The process of the application for summons would take some weeks, giving the wife the time to have second thoughts.

If the wife is reluctant and the law thinks she should give evidence against her spouse, she can be made to attend court and be treated as a hostile witness. The prosecution can then compare what she says in court with the statement she made at the time of the assault, and the magistrates, or jury in a High Court, can draw their own conclusions. You may wonder, however, how many marriages would be irrevocably ruined if we used these sledgehammer tactics. Although the law is there, should we leave it to the wife to judge what she should say, or should we guide her feet along a certain path because she may be afraid to speak the truth and needs the protection of the law? The police, with their knowledge gained in the school of experience, would undoubtedly differ from others in their decision.

Conclusion. Careful thought should guide our actions. Why, I wonder, do many people feel we should back-pedal over cases of child abuse and that the parents responsible need help when they inflict what are sometimes dreadful injuries on their own children? Is this line of thought just fashionable at the moment? The same people feel that when a defenceless wife is battered, strong action should be taken by the police, the husband arrested and placed in the cells. Although the battered wife is capable of taking action in her own defence, both physically and later verbally, the battered child is often too young to speak, though cruelly injured beyond words. It is recognised that in the case of the child he can be removed from home under a place of safety order and, eventually, a care order. Many children, though, are returned home by both social workers and magistrates to face further atrocities. Have we got our priorities right?

All too often social workers, doctors, nurses, health visitors and others see a child as a victim of an adult, perhaps in a minor way; we as police officers see them eventually on a post-mortem table in the mortuary. Can you blame us if our view is coloured, perhaps on occasions too much, by our concern for the welfare and protection of the child? We do not deliberately set out to break up the family unit. Our primary concern is for the health and well-being of the children in the family. It has only recently been recognised that children have rights and that someone should speak for them. If there is one group that has tried to do this over the years it is the police service.

It appears to be quite easy to pass legislation. To enforce it is another matter. We all have experienced legislation passed without proper facilities for its efficient implementation. The facilities required are what we should be agitating for, especially accommodation and readily available treatment, to assist people to stand on their own feet eventually.

Probably the most important thing we must seek is mutual trust between all those of us who desire to help less fortunate beings. We may be doctor, social worker, probation officer, teacher, nurse, police officer; our vocational instinct is to help our fellows, yet how can we do this if we do not trust and co-operate with each other? The only people who will lose if we fail will not be ourselves (if we discount the loss of a little professional dignity on occasions) but the people we are all trying to serve and help.

NOTE

[1]   *Common law* derives from custom passed down from time immemorial and administered in our courts, while *statute law* comprises Acts of Parliament or statutes. Quite often one finds that much common law has been incorporated into statute and that punishment is laid down by statute.

Tom Tomlinson   *Social worker*

8 INTER-AGENCY COLLABORATION: ISSUES AND PROBLEMS

Increasing concern is being expressed about the extent of violence in our society. Whether it is actually increasing or whether it is just becoming more overt is a question which the sociologist will have to answer. It is clear that concern about violence in the family has reached such a pitch that it cannot be ignored. Society as a whole has to make certain moral judgements concerning the control of violence, the management of the violent and the protection of those who are likely to be treated violently. There are clearly differing views concerning the causation and treatment of violence, and it may be that much more data will be needed before a clear picture will emerge. It is unlikely that any simple cause-and-treatment sequence will be found. Thus a concerted effort towards better understanding will have to be made by those agencies which have been delegated by society to treat violence and its side effects.

There are pressing situations at this moment that have to be dealt with even before adequate knowledge is available; and in addition to the lack of collated information concerning violence, the resources available to deal with its effects are also inadequate. Therefore it is essential that we make the best possible use of current resources and share any knowledge gained more effectively. There has been a great deal of discussion in the media about the difficulties caused for Social Services Departments by lack of manpower, high case loads and lack of residential facilities, both for children and for wives who have been subjected to violence. Wider issues of local authority planning have also come in for discussion, of particular note being the emotional and practical difficulties produced by local authority housing policies. These issues are under constant political consideration and it is perhaps significant that the agencies involved with violence are, to an increasing extent, becoming concerned with influencing social change and the allocation of resources. There is clearly a need for those who are involved to work towards the establishment of appropriate priorities in terms of resources available. This cannot be done effectively if the helping agencies remain isolated and constantly on the defensive. All too often, inter-agency communication means nothing more than an attempt on the part of one agency to force another agency to concede a point. This does not bring into question the sincerity of either agency, but I would suggest that it is to a large extent the result of systems stretched to the limit by the demands made on them. Therefore when a particular need is not met, blame is usually apportioned elsewhere. There is a clear case for improved communication between agencies and between the members of the same agency. I would therefore like to look at the concept of liaison, what it is for, and, if it seems to be so useful, why so little attention is devoted to it. One thing which became very clear during the preparation of this paper was the overwhelming importance of informal personal relationships with other people. It is, of course, important that some formal lines of communication are established. The procedural guidelines prepared jointly by some Social Services Departments and NSPCC special units are a good example of this. It would be very interesting, however, if research could demonstrate how much of the really useful collaborative work is done because of relationships which are built up informally.

As the theme of this book is physical violence in the family it is inevitable that most of the discussions centre on violence towards children and the beatings that wives are subjected to by their husbands or cohabitees. The Maria Colwell case brought a great deal of publicity to the problem of the non-accidentally injured child and highlighted many inadequacies in protection systems. The details are now well documented, and need not be repeated here. Suffice it to say that in the eight months before Maria died thirty-six complaints were made about her condition and fifty-six official visits were made by the welfare organisation involved and by the police. Misjudgement by social workers, pressure of work due to high case loads, lack of hard evidence on which to base police action were all held to contribute to the tragic outcome as well as the inadequate administrative systems that delayed vital messages and failed to follow up such matters as unkept school clinic appointments. The committee of enquiry reported that the need for better co-operation was clear; but exactly what is meant by co-operation, liaison or collaboration in this context? I should like to put forward a suggested definition. *Co-operation consists of the exchange and co-ordination of relevant information about a client in a potentially or actually dangerous situation, in order to decide upon an appropriate course of action.*

Fairly obvious, one might say! It is precisely because it seems so obvious that to leave the definition at that would be inadequate because of the different interpretations which each individual could apply to it. If the definition I have suggested is broadly accurate, then it gives rise to questions which need to be answered if the concept of co-operation is to be better understood. The ones posed below are not exhaustive but will perhaps serve to point out the ambiguities which still reside in this general definition.

How does one decide on what is a dangerous situation? Legal definitions may be unclear. The Children and Young Persons Act, 1969, gives general guidance on categories of children at risk but fails to define, for example, exactly what constitutes neglect, ill treatment, etc. In dealing with assaulted wives the differences between assault, wounding and grievous bodily harm would not be clear to most people outside the police service. Certainly one would have thought that the results of physical violence should be easy to measure, since one can see the results. However, it often takes a great deal of skill and knowledge such as that possessed by a paediatrician in order to determine which injuries are caused accidentally and which are not. Social workers often have even less clear-cut evidence on which to base decisions.

Who decides what information is relevant in these cases? Individuals are trained in their own particular skill. They may not be aware of the information that would be relevant to another agency, and hence may too easily define relevance in terms of their own agency and their own particular focus. For instance, the police may well see aggressive behaviour in a child as noteworthy but may ignore the fact that a child is withdrawn. To a social worker this withdrawal would be a clear indication that all was not well in the family. We are led to ask whether individual workers, especially those who are inexperienced, should be given responsibility for deciding what information is relevant and what constitutes a dangerous situation. Perhaps, as the people who are actually in contact with clients, they do it automatically, since their senior during supervision has to rely on the information offered by the worker to decide on the action which has to be taken. The agency has a clear responsibility to provide adequate supervision, especially for the large number of workers in Social Services Departments who are untrained. All too often, however, there is a lack of support from seniors owing to pressure of work, which would seem to be potentially dangerous. Questions need to be asked about the effectiveness of support systems in the agencies which are involved with family violence. How accessible, for example, is a senior social worker to the workers for whom he is responsible? If he is accessible, is his role that of a decision-maker, while the social worker puts the decisions into effect? Or does he use his position to act as a social work educator as well as a consultant? How much time does he spend with the social workers, going through the reasons for particular decisions rather than simply presenting them as a *fait accompli*? How much support does the inexperienced worker get from his senior during case conferences? Does the senior help the individual worker to clarify his own thoughts about the best course of action before going to a case conference?

These questions give some indication of the need for adequate training and post-training supervision. Unfortunately, what tends to happen at present is that a great deal of the work is done by untrained or recently trained workers. Although no one can deny their enthusiasm and sincerity, it could be argued that it is essential to continue supervisory help after training so that the individual worker can consolidate that training in the light of practice. If the worker is untrained, even more careful supervision is necessary — though one might question the advisability of untrained workers dealing with this kind of situation at all. There are occasions where untrained workers are simply left to get on with the job and the senior's function deteriorates into little more than dealing with the quantity rather than the quality of work undertaken. Moreover workers who have been trained are often promoted rapidly, without the necessary time to consolidate their training, and without even the experience of having their mistakes catch up on them, which is one way of learning.

Having raised some questions concerning practice, it might be now reasonable to query what *collaboration* is for. What purpose does it serve?

Firstly, it is useful for widening one's individual and collective knowledge of problems so that it can be related to the provision of current and future resources. In the long run this should enable the agencies concerned to allocate their resources more appropriately and also to plan for the future in a more constructive way. There is a great deal of valuable research information available which is simply not known to many social workers and others involved in this field. Work published by the NSPCC, articles that have appeared in medical journals and several continuing projects on violence in the family have become generally known only when workers get together to discuss current issues. Bringing them together also enables them to recognise their political function in that they can now be instrumental in trying to change policy. To this end there is a need for continual, on-going assessment of their methods of work and a responsibility to feed back through their agencies the actual needs of their clients.

Secondly, collaborative effort is part of the protective system of society. One immediately needs to ask who the protective system is intended for — the client or the agency? Ideally it should be for the benefit of the client. But it is perhaps a sad reflection on the efficiency of our systems that some method of formal checking on agency functioning has had to be devised. This has been rendered necessary not by lack of concern on the part of the people doing the work so much as by the shortage of resources stemming from society's indifference to the welfare of the disadvantaged.

There is also the human element to be considered, and no worker is infallible. Guidelines such as those set up by NSPCC special units and some local authorities provide a very good protection network, so long as they are implemented. A possible danger, however, in the establishment of formal systems is that this minimum standard is the one that everyone complies with. Further complications arise when one considers that collaborative effort can lead to intrusion into the freedom of both the client and the worker. In chapter 1 Professor Brandon makes the point that there are circumstances in which the parents' rights have to be sacrificed in favour of those of the child. Social workers are going to have to come to terms with the fact that they are agents of control within society as well as society's way of expressing concern. If, at case conferences, psychiatrists are called upon to give their professional opinion on the mental and paediatricians on the medical state of a child, then it is not unreasonable to ask social workers to give their professional opinion concerning family interaction and the child's social and emotional needs, even though this may limit the rights of other members of the family.

Thirdly, collaboration is also a means of determining when action needs to be taken and bringing the total resources available to bear upon the problem. This action may be related to an individual case, as in a case conference, or may be concerned with collective action, such as the setting up of a working party to discuss a wider problem — though it has to be recognised that the establishment of a working party may also be a device for shelving the problem and simply avoiding the need to take action for a time. When several agencies do consult over a given problem, how are decisions reached? Will the decision be that of the case conference or will the view of the individual agency already involved take precedence? If it is agreed that it is the case conference that is going to take the decision this may well involve conflict. The outcome will, of necessity, be a compromise between all the views represented at the conference, and there may be discrepancy between the decisions desired by one agency and those actually reached. The worker may be faced with having to accept a conference decision which his professional judgement tells him is wrong. In this connection problems also arise when chief officers override their representatives. For example, the police are often excluded from case conferences because of the fear that they will take unilateral action. Although chief constables of any authority have ultimate discretion, unless they can give an undertaking that their representatives will be bound by the decision of the conference the police contribution may be missing.

Why do the various agencies not collaborate more effectively if collaboration is regarded as useful and indeed essential? It would be as well to remind ourselves at the outset that collaboration between agencies and workers is based on personal relationships and that the quality of those relationships is determined by the attitude of the participants. When it is positive and reassuring, good collaboration can result even though the participants may start with essentially different viewpoints. Where the attitudes are destructively critical the participants become defensive and are disinclined to expose their own work and ideas to possible ridicule. This said, what sort of factors lead to inadequate collaboration?

Lack of knowledge of the function of other agencies, or even of what is required of oneself as a social worker, often plays a large part in liaison difficulties. It is a clear manifestation of lack of training and/or experience. Jean Renvoize, in her book *Children in Danger,* says that 30 per cent of all social workers are trained. It would be interesting to know how many of that 30 per cent are now engaged in administration, and how many of them who are still working at field level have had the opportunity to integrate theory and practice through supervision.

It is said that *pressure of work* may prevent people from collaborating. If this is the case it has implications for the employing bodies, who have to ensure that the workers are given the time to do their job properly. It may mean local authorities having to tell central government that there is no point in continuing to pass legislation which is politically expedient without giving them the resources to implement it. The implications do not affect only the employing body, as there is also a professional responsibility on the part of the individual worker to feed information back to that body. If he (or she) has reached a point where he no longer has time to think about what he is doing, then he ought to take a professional decision on what to do about it. Obviously, making a stand in isolation can be a very difficult thing to do, but it may ultimately be the only course open. A high turnover of staff may be a reflection of the conflict the workers are experiencing between their professional judgement and the pressures imposed by their responsibilities. Very often, pressure of work tends to be used as a defence because liaison exposes shortcomings of practice.

Another barrier to good collaboration is the *protection of status.* It occurs where there are real or assumed hierarchical differences between the people and agencies involved. The medical profession, for example, is based on a hierarchical structure and it would be very easy for a consultant to discount the views of a social worker because of her subordinate position in the hierarchy. It would be equally easy for the social worker to regard the consultant as out of touch with the social situation and concerned only with the medical side of his profession.

Many such instances of status difference can be discerned not only between but also within professions. Thus the trained and experienced social worker might be too ready to dismiss the ideas of those who are younger and perhaps less experienced, failing to see the enthusiasm and drive that makes them so persistent in trying to help with the problems that beset their clients. One may also look at group defences when considering the protection of status. Professional registers, for example, may be necessary to the improvement and protection of professional standards, but they also tend towards exclusivity and can encourage the creation of a 'mystique' which supposedly gives the registered member precedence when decisions are being reached. 'Professional status' in this case might lead some people to feel that his judgement cannot be questioned.

Confidentiality creates a lot of difficulty when it comes to considering how much information is to be exchanged with another agency. When people know another worker well and can exchange notes at an 'unofficial' level they are usually willing to pass on a good deal of data. On the other hand more caution may be necessary if a report is being submitted to a case conference which is going to be relatively public and official. Another difficulty which surrounds the whole issue of confidentiality centres on the fact that, in law, nobody except a client's barrister or solicitor has legal privilege. During an enquiry the court may order that any information an agency possesses shall be made public.

Rigidity of formal structures is another barrier to good co-operation. It may be very difficult to get to know workers in large organisations such as the police force, Departments of Health and Social Security, Social Services Departments, etc, because of the formal procedures which have to be gone through. The procedures may be essential for security reasons, and of themselves would not be so bad if there were some stability in the staffing situation, but turnover appears to be so fast in some organisations that no traditions of liaison can be built up.

Differences in aims between agencies or even workers in the same agency are another area of collaborative difficulty. In this situation common ground is almost coincidental and differences in aims may be either conscious or unconscious. For example, women's aid organisations, the police and Social Services Departments are all involved in cases of wife abuse but with differing ethical and political viewpoints. Women's Aid is concerned basically with the general emancipation of women; the police are concerned with social control aspects and the protection of the individual; while Social Services Departments would be concerned because of their role in caring for the disadvantaged. In this context extreme political differences are a real barrier to collaboration. Each side may be sincere in its own views but by their very nature may dismiss the viewpoint of others. It is important for all the agencies working in a field like this to be quite clear that they understand their own and others' motives. Social control agencies, for example, may need to learn that militant tenacity is necessary in order to achieve social change and that social change is vital for the survival of our society. Militant organisations for their part may have to learn that uncontrolled social change can be violent and destructive. People and agencies with a more middle-of-the-road view may be reluctant to associate with what they see as the more extreme organisations and thus avoid contact. Unfortunately, few of us see ourselves as being extreme, and so we do not really try to understand the viewpoint of others in a situation where all may be basically trying to grind their own axe. When confrontation replaces collaboration only statutory obligations tend to be fulfilled, and concessions are made as a reaction to extreme pressure. Inevitably the person or agency that has been faced with an aggressive stance is likely to respond in kind when its co-operation is needed.

The present relationships between social workers and social security workers, between police and social workers, and so on, may all be the result of either good collaboration or confrontation. It is interesting that where formal liaison schemes have been set up there appears to be a better understanding of the problems the other organisations face. Relationships tend to be better, and this ultimately makes it easier to help the client.

Workers' own ethics and feelings may hinder effective liaison. In this context it is interesting to ask whether our choice of work reflects our own needs. For instance, are social workers basically mediators because they are perhaps a little frightened of aggression? Because of this do they tend to avoid involvement in violent situations and exercise authority only with great reluctance? It would be equally interesting to know how far some of those who work in agencies that are involved with social control do so because they seek an outlet for their own aggression or are, possibly, afraid of change. Training may then reinforce a personal predisposition. For instance, the police are trained to be decisive, to take spot decisions about difficult situations. Social workers, on the other hand, are trained to leave decision-making until the last possible moment so that the maximum amount of evidence is available for making the decision. They sometimes complain that the police are heavy-handed. Conversely it often seems to the policeman that social workers are too hard to pin down.

The way in which conflict with social norms is viewed can also be a barrier to good collaboration. It may be that an individual client's coping mechanisms may be anti-social. A divorced woman who is on her own with young children may reach a point when she is under so much pressure that she can no longer tolerate the demands the children make on her. When things get to this pitch the children may be at risk. If her way of coping is to remove herself from the situation and leave them alone in the house it may result in her breaking the law, since her action might constitute neglect. How often do social workers insist that the woman stays with the children and threaten sanctions if she leaves them again? How would other professionals view and deal with this problem? A teenage boy may well be bottling up a lot of aggression against a very authoritarian father; maybe he copes with it by smashing bus shelters rather than letting his feelings build up to a point where he reacts explosively and attacks his father. A child who steals repeatedly to try and bring some sort of attention to his own misery is coping with the problem in an anti-social way. The social worker may perceive the meaning behind the act but consider it unlikely that the police would sympathise. There have to be limits to the degree of acceptable behaviour and the fact remains that however much one wishes to understand the individual, and his motives for any given behaviour, when he becomes a danger to others they must clearly be protected.

It is interesting, however, to look at the sort of reaction that anti-social clients elicit from society. Does society, for instance, tend to punish offences against material possessions more rigorously than those against the person?

These, then, are some of the issues raised when we are looking at the concept of interprofessional collaboration. What conclusions can be drawn from the points that have been discussed?

1   It needs to be recognised that there are ethical and political differences between workers and agencies. It is dangerous to assume that we all mean the same thing when we use the same words or even that we all want to achieve the same thing.
2   Status differences between those involved in this area can be largely artificial and may lead to the dismissal of a valid viewpoint. It would be interesting to know how many Directors of Social Services, for example, ever meet their basic grade social workers and ask their opinion directly

rather than through the intervening administrative structure. Social workers in turn have to recognise that their viewpoint is only one of many which a Director may have to take into consideration when making decisions.

3   People dedicated to change may have to recognise that uncontrolled change is destructive. Equally, enforcement agencies may need to see that change is essential for the survival of our society.

4   Sheer lack of knowledge and/or experience can be countered only by adequate training and supervision. This, inevitably, costs money. A greater emphasis on the education of the wider community in current social problems would be a good investment if it meant that society became less reluctant to pay for the service it wants.

5   Central government needs to re-examine its tendency to pass politically expedient legislation requiring already overloaded agencies to do even more work at a point in time when resources are actually being cut in real terms. The anxiety created by this sort of situation reduces the agencies' ability to cope even at the original level.

6   Some effort needs to be made to achieve stability of staffing in organisations so that liaison traditions can be built up. The emphasis at the moment appears to be largely on the establishment of new systems and laws. It could well be that greater stability and a chance to consolidate existing systems would be more productive.

Finally it should be emphasised that most useful collaboration goes on at an informal level, since it is only in getting to know other workers and agencies that suspicion and mistrust are reduced. At present little time seems to be allowed for workers to make informal contact with colleagues in other agencies, and most of the contact tends to be at senior officer level. Improving collaboration lower down the scale would mean reducing work loads and therefore increasing the number of social workers needed to provide a given service. If this is regarded as necessary it is going to cost money, and that money can be obtained only from the general community through higher taxation.

Index